Rhubarb Renaissance

D1446459

Rhubarb Renaissance

A Cookbook
by Ann Saling

Pacific Search Press

Pacific Search Press
222 Dexter Avenue North, Seattle, WA 98109
© 1978 Illustrations by Pacific Search Press
© 1978 by Ann Saling. All rights reserved
Printed in the United States of America

Second printing 1979
Third printing 1981

Designed by Paula Schlosser
Illustrated by Darci Covington

Library of Congress Cataloging in Publication Data

Saling, Ann.
    Rhubarb renaissance.
    Includes index.
    1. Cookery (Rhubarb). I. Title.
TX803.R58S44   641.6'5'48   77-29214
ISBN 0-914718-31-2

Contents

Introduction 9

Growing Rhubarb 11

Preparing and Cooking Rhubarb 14

Canning, Freezing, and Drying Rhubarb 17

Appetizers, Beverages, Breads, and Breakfasts 19

Soups, Sandwiches, and Salads 37

Vegetables, Sauces, and Stuffings 55

Relishes and Jams 71

Main Dishes 79

Desserts 111

Index 157

Acknowledgments

Many thanks to the following who contributed rhubarb
from their gardens: Fred Burk, Maude Simonton, the
Al Johnsons, Rick Saling, the Ed Colberts, Ann
Wilson, the Ira Springs, and Virginia Kammeyer.

Special thanks go to the Washington Rhubarb
Growers Association of Sumner for their cooperation,
their rhubarb donations, and their suggestions for
recipes.

And a fervent thank you to the resident taste-tester,
who stayed with it to the sweet-sour end — my
husband, Fred.

Introduction

Rhubarb is long overdue for a renaissance of popularity. It is one of the easiest food crops to grow, one of the most prolific and long-lasting producers (yielding for many years from the same roots), and one of spring's earliest vegetable harvests. Whether it is used in pies, entrées, or beverages, its puckery tartness and distinctive texture are a welcome change for winter-jaded palates.

Despite these desirable characteristics, rhubarb did not become part of the world's diet until the 1800s. Since 2700 B.C. when the Chinese began using it, rhubarb had been valued only for its medicinal properties. Centuries ago, Arab traders and Rhadonite Jews from Bagdad so valued the root for its purgative and astringent qualities that they went in caravans to seek it out in China. Marco Polo wrote, "Throughout all the mountainous parts of Succuir, the most excellent kind of rhubarb is produced in large quantities, and the merchants who come to buy it, convey it to all parts of the world." He also commented on seeing rhubarb growing "in the highest perfection" in the mountains near what is now called Soochow.

Rhubarb was known in Europe by at least the fourteenth century, but its use was still limited either to medicine or ornamental beauty. As late as 1810, a brave market gardener failed in an attempt to sell it on the London food market. But soon after, rhubarb made its debut as a culinary delicacy and became one of the most popular pie and tart ingredients in England. In some areas it is still called "pie plant" or "wine plant."

Humans cannot eat all types of rhubarb, however. The garden variety of rhubarb — *Rheum rhaponticum* — for example, is the only edible variety of some two dozen species of *Rheum* that are native to China, Siberia, and the Himalayas. Rhubarb grows in many other areas of the world as well, and many languages have similar words for it: *rhabarber* (German), *rabarber* (Swedish), *ruibarbo* (Spanish), *rabarbara* (Italian), and *rhubarbe* (French). *Barb* is derived from the Greek name for rhubarb, which means "something that comes from the barbarian country of Rha." (*Rha* is their word for the Volga River, along the shores of which rhubarb is abundant.)

The first mention of rhubarb in American literature was in 1778. Some say it was brought from Scotland. In any case, it soon became popular with the colonists as the first fresh "fruit" (it is actually a vegetable) available in the spring. An American cookbook published in the 1830s includes a recipe for rhubarb pie. Americans also used the plant as a medicine. A nineteenth-century book of home formulas lists rhubarb in various forms: pills, tinctures, syrups, and extracts. Some people still value its medicinal properties today.

Besides its medicinal and culinary uses, rhubarb was, for centuries, used as a source of poison. Both leaves and roots can be fatal to livestock and humans because of the large amounts of soluble oxalic acid they contain. (The stalks have only a small amount, which is insoluble and thus harmless.) During food shortages in World War I, the British government recommended eating the leaves but quickly retracted the recommendation after several deaths resulted.

The giant leaves, which extend more than two feet in diameter, are not totally useless, however. They were once worn inside the bonnets of midwestern farm women as extra protection against sunstroke. The leaves also make excellent compost, although they tend to mat and must be shredded before they are added to the compost pile.

Growing Rhubarb

Rhubarb's crimson stalks and huge, ruffled, dark green leaves make it an attractive addition to any garden whether it is used in a flower bed, in a vegetable garden, or close to the house as a foundation planting. It is not affected by most plant diseases and pests, except for slugs and snails. Because you will be eating the rhubarb stalks, do not use toxic sprays on nearby plants.

Rhubarb can be grown almost anywhere in the United States (except in the hottest, driest regions), but because it thrives in cool, moist areas, most of the commercial crop is grown in the northern third of the United States. It also grows well in the mountains in southern states even though it prefers winters cold enough to freeze the ground three or four inches deep. Commercial crops of rhubarb are grown in New England, the Great Lakes and Great Plains areas, and in the Pacific Northwest. Approximately ninety percent of the nation's hothouse rhubarb is grown in Washington State's moist, fertile Puyallup Valley; thirty percent of all rhubarb consumed in the United States is also grown there. Each year, rhubarb is a million dollar crop in Washington State.

In home gardens, rhubarb will yield each spring for ten or twelve years, even when completely neglected. When planted in rich, loose, sandy loam that is well manured and when given proper care, it will produce stalks two feet or more in length. When uncut, hothouse rhubarb may grow stalks more than six feet long.

Rhubarb is almost always propagated by root division, which is quicker and more reliable than planting seed. In order to maintain the quality and quantity of stalks, divide the roots every four to eight years, even though they will continue producing without being divided. Divide them after they have stopped producing — during the dormant season from late November to early spring. Dig root clumps and use an ax or sharp shovel to cut each clump into eight or twelve parts. Discard the older center part. Be sure there is a bud or "eye" in each section and as many feeder roots as possible. For extra protection, dust the cut pieces with a fungicide before replanting.

Because you will not be replanting and renewing the soil around the rhubarb root for a number of years, carefully prepare the soil for the new root sections. Planting holes should measure several feet across and three to four feet apart in all directions. Put coarse sand in the bottom, and then a layer of leaf mold, peat moss, or compost. Into this, mix some well-rotted manure or one-half cup of commercial fertilizer (5-10-5 or 5-10-10). Cover this mixture with good soil and place the root section on top; spread out the feeder roots. Cover the root with topsoil until there is not more than an inch or two of soil above the red buds on the clump. Then protect the plant with a layer of mulch. If you buy roots, plant them in the spring in the same manner.

Once planted, rhubarb requires little care, but it is a heavy feeder, requiring a mulch of compost and manure in the fall and a generous blanket of manure in late spring and summer. It prefers a moist but well-drained soil; full sun is not required.

During the first year of growth, do not harvest stalks from new plants because the roots still need to be nourished; during the second year, remove only the largest stalks. After that, you may liberally harvest the stalks, although a fourth of them should always be left on the plant at each picking. Promptly remove any flower stalks that develop.

Always pull stalks — do not cut them. Grip each stalk firmly and pull with a twisting motion so that the stalk pulls out cleanly. Crown rot can develop if any stumps are left above the ground. When you trim off the leaves, be sure to leave a "crow's foot" of leaf an inch or two long so the rhubarb will stay fresh longer.

Hothouse growers force their winter crop of rhubarb. They grow special fields of "mother plants" outdoors for two or three years, and do not cut any stalks; the roots are thus able to store up energy. From these fields, the growers dig huge root clumps, which they place on dirt floors inside dark, insulated field houses that are heated from fifty-two to fifty-five degrees Fahrenheit. Soon after they spray the roots with a growth hormone, pale pink stalks with underdeveloped, yellow green leaves shoot up. Because all the plant energy used to develop the stalks comes from the roots, the roots are exhausted at the end of the three-month harvest. They are then discarded.

Amateur growers can imitate this procedure. Allow several root clumps to go unharvested and then dig them up in December. Bring them into a dark basement area where the temperature stays around fifty-five degrees Fahrenheit. Roots will also produce when placed under greenhouse benches. The stalks will be slimmer than commercially grown hothouse rhubarb but just as succulent.

You can get an early harvest in your garden by heavily mulching plants with straw in the fall and covering them in January or February with a wooden box that light cannot penetrate. Or, when leaves first appear, cover the plant with a wooden box, the ends of which have been removed. Top the box with glass or clear plastic to retain heat. In either case, heap fresh manure against the sides of the box to create extra heat. (Never use fresh manure directly on plants.)

Preparing and Cooking Rhubarb

Most recipe books either ignore rhubarb or list only a few simple pie, jam, and dessert recipes, yet the delicious crimson stalk of rhubarb has a wide range of other uses. Its tartness and texture improve many sauces, cake icings, and sweet-sour dishes, and combine well with strawberries and citrus fruits. Some of the unusual recipes in this book pair rhubarb with cheese, avocado, chocolate, and green pepper.

Besides being distinctive in taste and versatile in use, rhubarb is also very low in calories — only fifty-six to the pound. In addition, it contains some valuable minerals (calcium, phosphorous, magnesium, and potassium) as well as some important vitamins (folic acid, niacin, pantothenic acid, riboflavin, and thiamine).

Field-grown rhubarb is at its succulent best in early spring. Commercial growers stop harvesting at the end of May because of their high standards, but homegrown rhubarb yields edible stalks, if regularly harvested, almost until the first frost arrives. Just leave a few stalks to nourish the roots.

Rhubarb's reputation has been tarnished by our tendency to overcook it. The stewed mush that has paraded as rhubarb sauce in the past bears no resemblance to the delicately flavored fruit that results from proper cooking. When prepared and cooked by the method recommended in this section, each bit of fruit stays whole and is intensified in color and flavor. Once you try this method, you will never go back to your former way of cooking rhubarb.

Preparing Rhubarb Sauce

A pound of raw rhubarb will yield about two cups of cooked sauce and about three and three-quarters cups of finely diced fruit. Once you have calculated the amount you need, split the stalks lengthwise before dicing. (Rhubarb that is finely diced need not be peeled.) Even the smallest stalks should be split in half; the larger ones should be split four to six times. Then pile up the cut stalks on a board and slice them about one-quarter inch wide. This prevents any stringiness, even in fairly mature rhubarb.

Before cooking, add sugar or honey, and let the diced fruit stand in it for at least an hour; several hours are better and overnight is best. (Be sure to stir the mixture occasionally.) This process draws out the juices and dissolves the sugar so that you do not need to add liquid for cooking the rhubarb. Add a few tablespoons of wine or fruit juice before cooking sauce that is to be used unsweetened, or for sweetened sauce that needs a special flavor.

The proportion of sugar to fruit you use is a matter of taste and calories. For a tart sauce, use one cup of sugar or honey to four cups of fruit. For a sweeter sauce, use almost twice that amount of sugar: three-fourths to one cup for each two cups of diced fruit. Jams, of course, take more sugar, and so do very rich dessert sauces. In meat dishes, cakes, and breads, sauce can often be used unsweetened. The distinctive flavor comes through better when rhubarb is tart enough to announce its presence. Dietetic sweeteners can be used, too.

Always be careful not to overcook rhubarb, especially hothouse rhubarb. Quickly bring the diced, sweetened fruit to a boil, then remove the pan from the heat and cover it. Let it stand a few minutes until the rhubarb softens. If it is not quite soft enough, put the pan over the heat again, and bring it just to the point of simmering. More liquid will form when you use more sugar. This delicious syrup should be drained off after cooking whenever drained sauce is called for in a recipe. This syrup can be added to fruit juices, especially orange juice, to enhance their flavor. For convenience, make up a quart or two of cooked sauce and keep it in the refrigerator so that you have some on hand when a recipe calls for a small amount.

There are two other ways to cook rhubarb so that the texture is mealy instead of mushy. Cook it in the top of a covered double boiler over boiling water for about fifteen minutes, with or without sugar, and without stirring. No liquid is needed. Or bake it, also without water, in a greased, covered shallow pan in a 300° oven for thirty minutes or more. Experiment to see which method you prefer. But always dice it fine first and presoak it in sugar or honey if you want it sweetened. You can also add a little (but not too much) grated orange peel, cinnamon, nutmeg, or ginger.

Hothouse rhubarb — available from January to March — is juicier than field-grown rhubarb, so when using it in a recipe where extra liquid might cause trouble, increase the thickening or use less rhubarb. (This rhubarb also cooks up much softer than the field-grown stalks.) Raw rhubarb keeps well in the refrigerator for a week or two, but moisten it occasionally. It is at its best, of course, just after it is picked.

If the rhubarb lacks color, add a few tablespoons of beet purée to intensify the red. Use baby food or whirl some cooked beets in a blender. Freeze the excess in ice cube trays and bag the cubes in plastic so you can use them later. Homegrown and fresh beets are especially sweet, and their flavor blends well with rhubarb.

Preparing Rhubarb Purée

When recipes call for purée, cook the sauce for five to ten minutes until the fruit is very soft. Then pass it through a food mill, whirl it in a blender, or press it through a food sieve.

Preparing Rhubarb Juice

When rhubarb juice is called for, prepare it as follows. Dice six cups of rhubarb. Simmer it in four cups of water until it is tender (about ten minutes). You can adjust the richness of the juice by adding more or less fruit or liquid. Let the mixture cool to lukewarm and then squeeze the juice through a double thickness of cheese-cloth; or substitute a muslin or flannel bag. Add one cup of sugar, honey, or corn syrup to the juice and reheat to boiling. Cool and chill. You can use this juice in punch, as a refreshing drink by itself (with a little lemon juice added), or in combination with other fruit juices. You can also make it in liquidizers that remove pulp, but because of the rhubarb fibers, you must chop stalks into small pieces before adding them to the liquidizer.

Canning, Freezing, and Drying Rhubarb

You can easily capture spring in a bottle by preserving rhubarb jam and juice. When canning, be sure to process the sealed jars full of boiling hot fruit or juice in a boiling water bath for a good ten minutes for safety's sake.

You can freeze rhubarb either raw or cooked. Cut the raw stalks into any convenient length (or even leave them whole) and bag them in plastic. When you want to use the stalks, cut them to the proper size while they are still slightly frozen. When using frozen rhubarb in such recipes as cakes, cookies, and breads, do not allow the rhubarb to thaw completely; use it as soon as you can break it up with a fork. Commercially frozen rhubarb, which is usually cut in one-half-inch pieces, can be chopped smaller while still partially frozen. If your frozen rhubarb is sweetened, be sure to cut down on the amount of sugar in the recipe.

Rhubarb sauce that is prepared as recommended in this book can also be frozen. When thawed, it will have the same taste and texture as freshly made sauce.

You can dry rhubarb in a dehydrator, but be sure first to cut the rhubarb into one-half-inch pieces. To use the dried pieces in cakes or breads, soak them in water until soft. Then sweeten the water and drink the refreshing juice.

However you have prepared and used rhubarb in the past, you can begin now to enjoy using rhubarb creatively in a wide range of culinary delicacies. The Rhubarb Renaissance is certainly long overdue.

Appetizers,
Beverages,
Breads,
and
Breakfasts

Indonesian Vegetable Dip

Cream cheese 1 8-ounce package at room temperature
Unflavored yogurt 1 cup
Rhubarb sauce (see Index) 1 cup sweetened and drained
Curry powder 1 tablespoon
Soy sauce 2 to 3 teaspoons

Whip the cream cheese, and blend in other ingredients. Makes about 3 cups.

Fresh Fruit Smorgasbord Dip

Sour cream 1 cup
Rhubarb sauce (see Index) ¼ cup sweetened and drained
Shredded coconut ¼ cup
Almonds ¼ cup sliced
Lemon juice 1 tablespoon
Rhubarb syrup drained from sauce

Mix all ingredients together, adding rhubarb syrup until dip is proper consistency. Delicious with banana slices (for a scalloped look, run a fork down the sides before slicing), fresh pineapple spears, whole strawberries, melon balls, or seedless grapes. Makes about 1½ cups.

Puget Sound Special

Cream cheese   1 8-ounce package at room temperature
Dillweed   ½ teaspoon
Chives   1 tablespoon finely snipped
Onion   1 tablespoon finely grated
Lemon juice   1 tablespoon
Tabasco sauce   2 drops
Smoked salmon, trout, or turkey   ½ cup
Rhubarb sauce (see Index)   3 tablespoons slightly sweetened and
    drained
Crackers or toast rounds

Whip the cream cheese until fluffy. Gradually whip in next 7 ingredients; chill. Serve as a spread with crackers. Makes about 1½
cups.

Egg Spread Exotique

Eggs   2 hard-cooked and chopped
Rhubarb purée (see Index)   3 tablespoons unsweetened
Capers   1 teaspoon
Prepared mustard   ½ teaspoon
Soy sauce   ½ teaspoon
Green onions with tops   2 tablespoons chopped
Tarragon vinegar   2 tablespoons
Paprika   ½ teaspoon
Walnuts   2 tablespoons chopped
Cream cheese   1 3-ounce package, whipped fluffy
Salt   to taste
Canapé bread, thin ham slices, or lettuce leaves

Mix first 10 ingredients together, adding salt as needed. Spread on
canapé bread, or roll up in ham slices or lettuce leaves secured with
toothpicks and cut into bite-size pieces. Makes about 1 cup.

Lemony Tuna-Barb Spread

Cream cheese   1 8-ounce package at room temperature
Tuna   1 6½-ounce can drained and flaked
Rhubarb sauce (see Index)   ¼ cup unsweetened and drained
Onion   2 tablespoons minced
Prepared horseradish   1 to 2 teaspoons
Tarragon   ½ teaspoon crumbled
Lemon juice   1 teaspoon
Lemon peel   1 teaspoon grated
Green pepper   2 tablespoons finely minced
Pimiento   1 tablespoon minced
Celery sticks, cucumber rounds, canapés, or fresh vegetables

Whip cream cheese until fluffy. Blend in next 9 ingredients, adjusting flavorings to taste. Keep mixture quite stiff. Use spread on celery sticks, cucumber rounds, or canapés, or as a vegetable dip. (To thin, add more rhubarb sauce.) Makes about 2 cups.

Beanbarb Bash

Pork and beans   1 cup drained
Onion   ⅓ cup coarsely chopped
Rhubarb sauce (see Index)   ⅓ cup unsweetened and drained
Prepared mustard   2 teaspoons
Molasses   1 teaspoon
Worcestershire sauce   1 teaspoon
Bacon slices   3, fried crisp and crumbled
Crackers or fresh vegetables

Whirl first 6 ingredients in blender until smooth; stir in bacon. Use crackers or fresh vegetables to dip in sauce. Makes 1⅔ cups.

Chafing Dish Mustard Dip

Rhubarb sauce (see Index)   1 ½ cups moderately sweet
Orange juice   ¼ cup
Prepared mustard   1 tablespoon
Onion   2 tablespoons minced
Tarragon vinegar   1 tablespoon
Green pepper   2 tablespoons minced
Cocktail sausages, wiener rounds, or cubed canned ham   3 cups

Mix all ingredients but meat; simmer in a skillet for a few minutes to blend. Add meat and simmer gently for 15 minutes or more. Then transfer to a chafing dish. Provide cocktail picks for spearing meat. Makes 2 cups.

Ham and Celery Stuffer

Cream cheese   1 3-ounce package at room temperature
Peanut butter   ⅓ cup
Rhubarb sauce (see Index)   ⅓ cup moderately sweet and drained
Peanuts   ¼ cup chopped
Bacon slices   2, fried crisp and crumbled
Worcestershire sauce   2 teaspoons
Salt   to taste
Celery stalks   8 to 10 or
    Thin ham slices   6 boiled

Mix first 7 ingredients together. Use to stuff celery or to put in center of ham slices, which are then rolled up, secured by cocktail toothpicks, and cut in bite-size pieces. Makes 18 from 6 ham slices. Makes 1 ¼ cups thick sauce.

Rhubi Supercooler

Rhubarb sauce (see Index)   1 cup sweetened or
    Dessert Sauce au Vin (see Index)   1 cup
Ice   2 cups chopped
Powdered milk   ¼ cup (optional)
Fresh mint   garnish

Whirl first 3 ingredients in blender until slushy with no large bits of
ice remaining. Garnish with sprig of mint and drink at once. Any
extra can be frozen for Popsicles, but be sure ice is ground fine.
Serves 2.

Passionate Pink Punch

Rhubarb   8 cups diced
Water   4 cups
Honey or sugar   about 2 cups
Frozen orange juice concentrate   1 12-ounce can
Lemon juice   ¼ cup
Strong tea   2 cups, chilled
Ginger ale   1 quart bottle, chilled
Fresh mint   garnish
Strawberries   cut into slices

Simmer rhubarb in water for about 10 minutes. Press through sieve
or jelly bag. If you use sugar, heat juice to dissolve sugar well; chill.
Add other juices and tea; chill. Add ginger ale just before serving.
Garnish each glass with a sprig of fresh mint and some strawberry
slices. Makes about 3 quarts.
Variation: For 3 servings use 1 cup rhubarb juice, 1 cup orange
juice, 1 tablespoon lemon juice, and 2 cups ginger ale.

Mock Pink Champagne

Rhubarb juice (see Index)   1 cup sweetened and chilled
Dry white wine   2 cups, chilled
Ginger ale   1 quart bottle, chilled

For each glass, use 4 tablespoons rhubarb juice, stirred well into ½ cup wine. Fill glass with ginger ale. Serves 4.

Pink Pearl Froth

Rhubarb juice (see Index)   2 cups slightly sweetened
Pineapple juice   ¾ cup
Lemon juice   2 tablespoons
Egg white   1
Ginger ale   1 cup (optional)
Fresh mint sprigs   garnish

Mix first 4 ingredients together and whisk to raise a slight foam. Add ginger ale for sparkle if desired. Top with a fresh mint sprig. Makes almost 1 quart.

California Waker-Upper

Prune juice   1 cup, chilled
Rhubarb juice (see Index)   1 cup sweetened and chilled*
Unflavored yogurt   1 cup, chilled
Honey   ¼ cup
Egg   1
Powdered milk   ⅓ cup

Whirl all ingredients in blender or beat with rotary beater until frothy and well mixed. Serves 4.

*You can substitute liquid drained from sauce used in other recipes.

Pine-Barb Shake

Rhubarb sauce (see Index) 1 cup slightly sweetened with honey
Pineapple juice 1 cup, chilled
Unflavored yogurt 1 cup, chilled
Milk ½ cup, chilled
Pineapple sherbet or vanilla ice cream 1 cup

Beat all ingredients with rotary beater only until mixed, or whirl briefly in blender. Serves 4.
Variation: Freeze the shake until slushy in freezing compartment of refrigerator, but not in ice cube compartment. Use for cake or pudding "a la mode" sauce.

Eggstra Good Eggnog

Egg 1, separated
Honey 1 tablespoon
Milk ¾ cup, well chilled
Unflavored yogurt ½ cup, well chilled
Vanilla ¼ teaspoon
Rhubarb purée (see Index) ¼ cup sweetened
Nutmeg ⅛ teaspoon

Beat yolk with whisk until creamy. Stir in honey, milk, yogurt, vanilla, and purée. Beat egg white until stiff; fold into milk mixture. Pour into 2 glasses and sprinkle nutmeg on top. Serves 2.
Variation: For a traditional variation, replace milk with cream, and add bourbon and rum to taste.

In-the-Pink Health Drink

Pineapple juice 1 cup
Zucchini 1 cup diced
Rhubarb sauce (see Index) ⅓ cup sweetened

Whirl all ingredients in blender until well liquidized. Serves 2 to 3.

Rosy Rhubarb Liqueur

Red rhubarb stalks   2 cups very finely diced
Sugar   2 cups
Vodka   ½ fifth

Let rhubarb stand in sugar for several hours until sugar is dissolved. Simmer it gently just to finish dissolving, but do not cook rhubarb; cool. Add to vodka in a quart jar. Let it stand for several days, shaking it occasionally. Remove rhubarb and save it for a dessert recipe. Liqueur will be a rosy color. Serves 8.

Springtime Breakfast Bread

Flour   1 cup sifted
Sugar   2 tablespoons
Salt   ½ teaspoon
Baking powder   1½ teaspoons
Baking soda   ½ teaspoon
Margarine   ¼ cup
Egg   1, beaten
Milk   ⅓ cup
Vanilla   ½ teaspoon
Rhubarb sauce (see Index)   1 cup sweetened and drained
Strawberries   ½ cup frozen and thawed*
Brown sugar   ¼ cup
Flour   3 tablespoons
Margarine   ¼ cup
Walnuts   ¼ cup, unchopped

Preheat oven to 400°. Sift together flour, sugar, salt, baking powder, and soda. Cut in margarine until mixture is crumbly. Combine egg, milk, and vanilla; add to dry ingredients and stir until moistened. Spread batter in greased 8-inch square baking pan. Mix rhubarb sauce and berries; spoon mixture over batter. Combine brown sugar and 3 tablespoons flour. Cut in margarine until crumbly. Sprinkle over fruit topping and top with nuts. Bake for 30 minutes.
*Fresh, halved strawberries may be substituted.

Cornbread à l'Orange

Flour 1 cup sifted
Baking powder 3 teaspoons
Baking soda ½ teaspoon
Salt ½ teaspoon
Sugar 2 tablespoons
Cornmeal ½ cup
Egg 1
Margarine 2 tablespoons, melted
Rhubarb sauce (see Index) ¾ cup unsweetened and drained
Frozen orange juice concentrate 3 tablespoons

Preheat oven to 350°. Sift first 5 ingredients together; mix in cornmeal. Mix remaining ingredients together. Stir rhubarb mixture into
dry ingredients; mix until just moistened. Spread the thick batter
evenly into a greased 8-inch square pan. Bake for 30 minutes.
Freezes well.

Brown Bread Bostonian

Wheat germ ¾ cup
Flour 1⅓ cups
Baking soda 1 teaspoon
Cloves ¼ teaspoon
Salt ¼ teaspoon
Molasses ½ cup
Rhubarb sauce (see Index) ⅓ cup slightly sweetened and drained
Raisins ¼ cup
Margarine ¼ cup
Honey ¼ cup
Egg 1

Spread wheat germ on cookie sheet and toast until golden (about 10
minutes) in 300° oven. Stir with spatula as edges brown. Sift dry ingredients together and mix with the toasted wheat germ. In a
separate bowl, mix molasses, rhubarb, and raisins. In a large bowl

cream margarine and honey; add egg and beat in. Add molasses mixture and dry ingredients alternately to margarine mixture; beat lightly after each addition. Pour into a greased 8-inch square pan. Bake at 350° for about 30 minutes. Cut in squares.

Note: This bread is delicious with baked beans, ham, etc.

Tea 'n' Coffee Bread

Brown sugar   1 cup
Eggs   2
Salad oil   ¾ cup
Instant coffee powder   1 tablespoon
Orange juice   ¼ cup
Whole wheat flour   1 cup
Flour   1 cup
Vanilla   2 teaspoons
Baking soda   1 teaspoon
Baking powder   2 teaspoons
Cinnamon   1 teaspoon
Salt   1 teaspoon
Nutmeg   ¼ teaspoon
Allspice   ¼ teaspoon
Rhubarb   1¼ cups finely diced
Lemon juice   1 tablespoon
Lemon peel   1 teaspoon grated
Unflavored yogurt   ¼ cup
Walnuts   1 cup chopped

Preheat oven to 325°. Mix all ingredients together in a large bowl. Pour batter into a greased 9 by 4-inch loaf pan with waxed paper on bottom; pour extra batter into greased muffin tins. Bake loaf for 50 to 60 minutes and cupcakes about 20 minutes.

Deviled Quick Bread

Margarine ¼ cup
Sugar ¼ cup
Egg 1
Whole wheat flour ½ cup
Rhubarb 1 cup finely diced
Flour ½ cup
Baking powder ½ teaspoon
Baking soda ½ teaspoon
Dry mustard 1 teaspoon
Salt ½ teaspoon
Milk 3 tablespoons
Cheddar cheese ¾ cup shredded
Walnuts ⅓ cup chopped

Preheat oven to 350°. Cream margarine and sugar; beat in egg; add whole wheat flour and rhubarb. Sift together other dry ingredients and then add them alternately with milk to egg mixture. Dough will be very stiff. Stir in cheese and nuts. Spread dough out in a greased 9 by 5-inch loaf pan. Bake for 40 to 45 minutes. Let stand for several hours before slicing. Delicious hot or cold, and keeps well.

Spice-of-Life Muffins

Rhubarb ¾ cup very finely diced
Honey 2 tablespoons
Flour 1¾ cups sifted
Sugar ½ cup
Baking powder 2 teaspoons
Baking soda ½ teaspoon
Salt 1 teaspoon
Cinnamon ½ teaspoon
Nutmeg ¼ teaspoon
Cloves ⅛ teaspoon
Eggs 2
Milk ½ cup
Orange juice ¼ cup
Molasses 2 tablespoons
Margarine ⅓ cup, melted*
Walnuts ¼ cup coarsely chopped

Drizzle honey over rhubarb and let stand for 1 hour or overnight. Sift together dry ingredients. Beat eggs; blend in milk, orange juice, molasses, margarine, and honey and rhubarb mixture; add to dry ingredients and stir lightly, only to mix; batter will be stiff. Spoon it into greased large cupcake tins until they are ⅔ full. Sprinkle nuts over top. Bake for about 25 minutes at 375°. Let stand in pan for a few minutes before removing. Makes 12.

*⅓ cup salad oil can be substituted.

Good Morning Coffee Cake

Brown sugar ¾ cup
Margarine ¼ cup
Orange peel ½ teaspoon grated
Egg 1, slightly beaten
Vanilla 1 teaspoon
Rhubarb sauce (see Index) ½ cup unsweetened and drained
Flour 1 cup sifted
Baking soda ½ teaspoon
Baking powder ½ teaspoon
Salt ¼ teaspoon
Unflavored yogurt ½ cup
Brown sugar ¼ cup
Flour ⅓ cup
Margarine 2 tablespoons
Pecans ½ cup chopped
Shredded coconut ¼ cup

Preheat oven to 350°. Cream sugar and margarine together. Add orange peel, egg, vanilla, and rhubarb sauce, blending well. Sift dry ingredients together. Add ½ to creamed mixture and blend. Add yogurt and mix well. Add other ½ of flour mixture and beat well. Pour into an 8-inch square pan with sides greased and bottom greased and floured. Mix rest of ingredients together and sprinkle over cake. Bake 40 minutes. Serve hot. Serves 6.

Ricky's Upside Downers

Rhubarb   1 cup finely diced
Sugar   1 cup
Orange peel   1 teaspoon grated
Margarine   ¾ cup (to be used in 3 parts)
Ginger   ½ teaspoon
Lemon juice   1 teaspoon
Flour   2 cups
Salt   1 teaspoon
Baking soda   1 teaspoon
Baking powder   1 teaspoon
Unflavored yogurt   1 cup
Brown sugar   4 tablespoons
Walnuts or pecans   ½ cup chopped

Let rhubarb stand in sugar an hour or overnight. Simmer gently with orange peel, ¼ cup margarine, ginger, and lemon juice until thick. Sift dry ingredients together. Cut in ¼ cup margarine and then quickly mix in yogurt to make a soft dough. Turn out on floured board; knead a couple of times. Then roll out in a rectangle. Spread with ¼ cup margarine and sprinkle with brown sugar. Roll up along the long side, pressing in the seam. Cut into 12 rolls. Put thick rhubarb mixture and nuts into greased muffin tins; add a roll, cut side up. Bake at 375° for about 20 minutes. Let stand for a few minutes before removing with a fork. Makes 12.

Busy Day Batter Buns

Dry yeast 1 package
Warm water ⅔ cup
Flour 1 cup
Sugar 2 tablespoons
Salt ½ teaspoon
Margarine ¼ cup soft
Egg 1 at room temperature
Flour ⅔ cup
Raisins ½ cup
Rhubarb ¾ cup finely diced

Sprinkle yeast over warm water. Mix together 1 cup flour, sugar, salt, margarine, and egg. Beat into water-yeast mixture for 2 minutes. Then add ⅔ cup flour, and beat for 1 minute. Add raisins and rhubarb and beat until well mixed. Spoon batter into greased muffin tins until they are ½ full. Cover with a clean dish towel and put in warm place to rise (over hot water heater, for example) for 45 minutes. When doubled in size, bake at 375° for 15 minutes. Makes 12 tender buns, which freeze well.

Broiled Breakfast Buns

English muffins   4, split and lightly toasted
Butter   to taste
Margarine   ½ cup soft
Brown sugar   ½ cup
Vanilla   1 teaspoon
Rhubarb sauce (see Index)   ⅓ cup sweetened and drained
Orange peel   1 teaspoon grated
Pecans or almonds   ½ cup coarsely chopped

Thickly spread muffin halves with butter. Mix together margarine
and sugar, creaming well. Add vanilla, rhubarb, and orange peel,
and blend. Spread mixture on muffin halves and then sprinkle with
nuts. Broil under broiler until bubbling hot. Makes 8 rich breakfast
buns.

Golden Glow French Toast

Whole wheat bread slices   6
Eggs   2, slightly beaten
Rhubarb purée (see Index)   ¼ cup sweetened
Milk   2 tablespoons
Vanilla   ¼ teaspoon
Orange peel   ½ teaspoon grated
Orange juice   ¼ cup
Salt   ⅛ teaspoon
Nutmeg   ⅛ teaspoon
Cheerios   ½ cup coarsely crushed
Margarine   ¼ cup, melted
Syrup or honey and butter

Preheat oven to 425°. Dip the bread into a mixture of the next 8 ingredients; let slices soak up liquid. Then press each slice on both
sides into crushed cereal. Place on greased baking sheet. Drizzle
margarine over top. Bake 8 to 10 minutes. Use a mild-flavored syrup
over the toast, or just honey and butter. Serves 3.

Hallelujah Hot Cakes

Whole wheat flour   ½ cup
Dry milk powder   ¼ cup
Salt   1 teaspoon
Cornmeal   ⅓ cup
Fine dry bread crumbs   1 cup
Egg   1
Salad oil   ¼ cup
Rhubarb sauce (see Index)   1 cup sweetened and not drained
Water   ½ cup

Mix all dry ingredients together thoroughly. Mix together egg, oil, rhubarb sauce, and water. Blend into dry mixture. Batter will be thick; add more water if necessary. Fry in buttered fry pan. Makes 12 pancakes.

Note: Since these cakes are thick, make them smaller than usual and let them cook longer. These cakes are so delicious they do not need to be smothered with syrup or jam. They can be frozen and reheated in toaster after thawing.

Hearty Scotch Breakfast

Quick cooking oats   ⅔ cup
Water   1¼ cups
Salt   ¼ teaspoon
Rhubarb sauce (see Index)   ⅓ cup sweetened with honey
Raisins   1 tablespoon
Walnuts   ¼ cup fairly finely chopped
Brown sugar   2 tablespoons or to taste
Margarine   1 tablespoon
Unflavored yogurt   ⅓ cup
Nutmeg   dash

Mix oats, water, salt, rhubarb sauce, and raisins in a saucepan. Bring to a boil, stirring occasionally; cook 1 minute. Remove from heat, cover pan, and let stand for a few minutes. Stir in walnuts, brown sugar, and margarine. Spoon yogurt over mixture and sprinkle with nutmeg. Serves 2.

Soups,
Sandwiches,
and
Salads

Double Surprise Soup

Onion   3 tablespoons chopped
Celery   ⅓ cup finely chopped
Bacon fat or margarine   3 tablespoons
Flour   2 tablespoons
Chicken broth   1½ cups
Peanut butter   ⅓ cup
Milk   1½ cups
Rhubarb   ⅓ cup very finely diced

Sauté onion and celery in bacon fat until onion is golden and soft; sprinkle flour over them and stir until smooth. Gradually stir in chicken broth. Mix in peanut butter and let simmer a few minutes. Add milk gradually until soup is proper consistency. Heat just to boiling point; add rhubarb and cook for only 1 minute. Serves 3 to 4.

Rhubarb Soup à la Zorba

Lamb shoulder roast   leftover bones from*
Cold water   enough to cover
Bay leaf   1
Peppercorns   3
Salt   to taste
Brown rice   2 tablespoons
Dillweed   ½ teaspoon
Onion   ¼ cup chopped
Rhubarb   ½ cup finely diced
Egg   1
Lemon juice   2 tablespoons

Simmer bones in water about 1 hour with bay leaf and peppercorns. Broth should be savory. Strain broth and add salt, rice, dillweed, and onion; simmer about 25 minutes or until rice is tender. Remove from heat; add rhubarb, cover, and let stand. Whip egg with lemon juice; stir into soup. Serve at once. Serves 4.
*Rich chicken broth can also be used.

Seafood Avocado Chiller

Large avocado   1, seeded, peeled, and chilled
Rhubarb sauce (see Index)   ½ cup unsweetened
Unflavored yogurt   ½ cup
Chicken broth   1½ cups seasoned to taste
Minced clams or shrimp   ½ cup drained
Curry powder   1 teaspoon (optional)
Garlic clove   1, minced
Worcestershire sauce   ½ teaspoon
Lemon juice   1 tablespoon
Bacon slices   3, fried crisp and crumbled
Cucumber   ½ cup peeled and chopped
Green onions with tops   ½ cup minced

Put first 9 ingredients into blender and whirl until blended. Pour into a bowl and stir in bacon and cucumber; chill well. Sprinkle green onions over top of each serving. Makes about 3 cups. Serves 4 to 5.

Viking Fruit Soup

Rhubarb   2 cups finely diced
Orange juice   ½ cup
Water   1 cup
Dry red wine   1 cup
Lemon juice   1 tablespoon
Orange rind   grated from 1 orange
Allspice   ½ teaspoon
Sugar   ¼ cup or more
Cornstarch   1 tablespoon
Cold water
Raisins   ¼ cup chopped
Whipping cream or sour cream   ½ cup
Lemon   4 to 6 slices
Cloves   4 to 6
Nutmeg   ¼ teaspoon

Simmer rhubarb with orange juice and water for 10 minutes or until soft; pass through food mill or sieve. Add wine, lemon juice, orange rind, allspice, and sugar to taste; reheat. Mix cornstarch with a little cold water and stir it into hot soup. Simmer until soup is clear and begins to thicken. Add raisins. Serve either hot or cold. To serve hot, stir whipping cream in and top each soup plate with lemon slice with a clove stuck in it; sprinkle with nutmeg. Or chill well, and top each serving with mound of whipped cream or sour cream. Add lemon slice and sprinkle with nutmeg. Serve before or after main course. Serves 4 to 6.

Chilled Chicken Delight

Chicken broth   2 cups rich, well seasoned
Rhubarb sauce (see Index)   3 cups sweetened and fairly liquid
Orange juice   1 cup
Unflavored yogurt   ½ cup
Fresh whole strawberries   6

Mix ½ of broth with rhubarb sauce in blender; whirl until frothy. Pour into bowl, add rest of chicken broth, orange juice, and yogurt. Beat with rotary beater until frothy; chill for several hours. Top each serving with a fresh strawberry. Serves 6.

Whipped Cream Cheese Sandwiches

Cream cheese   1 3-ounce package at room temperature
Rhubarb sauce (see Index)   ¼ cup sweetened and drained
Raisins   2 tablespoons chopped
Almonds or walnuts   ¼ cup very finely chopped
Lemon juice   1 teaspoon

Whip the cream cheese until fluffy; add other ingredients. Makes enough for 4 sandwiches.

Note: This is an excellent spread for fruit tea breads or molasses brown breads.

Cheesy Cucumber Open-Faces

Cucumber 1 cup peeled and diced
Onion 2 tablespoons grated
Unflavored yogurt ½ cup
Sharp cheddar cheese 1 cup shredded
Rhubarb sauce (see Index) ¼ cup slightly sweetened and drained
Prepared mustard 1 teaspoon
Tomato ½ cup finely diced and peeled
Salt ¼ teaspoon
Basil ¼ teaspoon crumbled
Rye or whole wheat bread slices 6

Mix all ingredients except bread together, being careful not to mash tomatoes. Toast bread and butter it; spread thickly with sandwich mix. Broil just until cheese is melted. Makes 6.

Note: This is also delicious spooned over cut wieners (plumped in hot water) and broiled.

Hearty Bacon 'n' Eggwich

Eggs 2, hard-cooked and chopped
Pitted black olives ⅓ cup sliced in rings
Green onions with tops 3 tablespoons minced
Swiss or cheddar cheese ⅔ cup shredded
Rhubarb sauce (see Index) 3 tablespoons slightly sweetened and drained
Mayonnaise ⅓ cup
Garlic salt ⅛ teaspoon
Savor salt ⅛ teaspoon
Coarsely ground black pepper ¼ teaspoon
Prepared mustard ½ teaspoon
Bacon slices 4 or more, fried crisp and crumbled
Rye or whole wheat bread slices 8 to 10

Mix everything together except bread; then spread on buttered toasted bread. Makes 4 to 5 sandwiches.

Note: This is also good for appetizers; spread it on crackers or toasted bread rounds.

After School Special

Margarine   1 tablespoon
Peanut butter   2 tablespoons
Rhubarb sauce (see Index)   4 tablespoons sweetened and drained
Lemon juice   1 teaspoon
Raisin bread slices   2

Mix all together and spread on toasted raisin bread. Makes 2 sandwiches.

Turkey Bombay

Cream cheese   1 3-ounce package at room temperature
Mayonnaise   ¼ cup
Green onions with tops   2 tablespoons minced
Green pepper   2 tablespoons minced
Rhubarb sauce (see Index)   ⅓ cup slightly sweetened and drained
Curry powder   to taste
Whole wheat bread slices   8, buttered
Turkey breast   4 thin slices, cooked
Salt   to taste
Pepper   to taste
Paprika   to taste

Cream together cream cheese, mayonnaise, onions, and green pepper; mix in rhubarb and curry powder. Spread this mixture on 4 slices of bread; add a slice of turkey to each and season. Top with other 4 slices and cut in ½. Makes 4 sandwiches.

Lo-Cal Cottage Sandwich

Lo-cal cottage cheese ⅓ cup
Rhubarb sauce (see Index) 3 tablespoons slightly sweetened and
    drained
Whole grain bread slices 4, buttered

Mix together cottage cheese and rhubarb. Spread on toasted bread
and broil for several minutes until steamy. Makes 4.

Layered Surprise

Rye or whole wheat bread slices 6
Margarine 6 tablespoons
Honey 6 tablespoons
Rhubarb sauce (see Index) 1 cup sweetened and drained
Boiled ham 6 slices
Prepared mustard 6 tablespoons
Swiss cheese 6 slices

Spread bread with margarine and honey. Top with a thin layer of
rhubarb sauce, and ham. Spread ham with mustard; top with
cheese. Broil until cheese is bubbly. Makes 6 open-face sandwiches.
Variation: Provide a top to the sandwich. Prepare a mixture of 2
beaten eggs with ⅓ cup milk. Dip sandwiches on both sides. Fry in
melted margarine until piping hot.

Tangy Chickenwich

Chicken meat   2 cups cooked and coarsely chopped
Rhubarb sauce (see Index)   1 cup slightly sweetened and drained
Mayonnaise   ¼ cup or enough to moisten mixture well
Green pepper   2 tablespoons finely minced
Onion   2 tablespoons minced
Almonds or walnuts   ¼ cup chopped
Rye or whole wheat bread slices   8 to 10, buttered

Mix all together well, except bread. Spread bread with filling.
Makes 4 to 6 sandwiches.

Peanut Butter Broil

Pork and beans   1 cup drained and mashed
Rhubarb sauce (see Index)   ⅓ cup unsweetened and drained
Green onions with tops   3 tablespoons chopped
Mayonnaise   ¼ cup
Whole wheat bread slices   6
Butter
Peanut butter   ½ cup
Cheddar cheese   ¼ cup shredded
Bacon slices   4, fried crisp and crumbled

Mix together beans, rhubarb, onions, and mayonnaise. Toast bread
lightly; spread with butter and peanut butter. Layer on bean
mixture. Sprinkle cheese over each sandwich and top with bacon.
Broil for a few minutes until piping hot and cheese is melted. Makes
6 hearty sandwiches.

Glorified Gobbler

English muffins   2, halved, toasted, and buttered
Rhubarb sauce (see Index)   ½ cup slightly sweetened and drained
Turkey   4 slices cooked
Turkey gravy or cream of chicken soup   2 cups
Swiss cheese   4 slices
Paprika   ⅛ teaspoon

Lay ½ of each muffin on a plate. Spread with rhubarb sauce; top with turkey; pour gravy over all. Lay a slice of cheese on top and broil until cheese melts. Sprinkle with paprika. Serves 4.

Tangy Tuna Toss

Tuna   1 6½-ounce can, drained and coarsely flaked
Eggs   2 hard-cooked and chopped
Celery   ⅔ cup finely chopped
Green onions with tops   ¼ cup chopped
Lemon juice   1 tablespoon
Salt   ¼ teaspoon
Coarsely ground black pepper   ⅛ teaspoon
Rhubarb sauce (see Index)   ½ cup slightly sweetened
Walnuts   1 cup coarsely chopped
Margarine   1 tablespoon, melted
Mayonnaise   ½ cup
Curry powder   ¼ teaspoon
Cabbage   2 cups finely shredded
Mayonnaise   ¼ cup

Mix first 8 ingredients together. Sauté walnuts in margarine for a few minutes; drain on paper towel. Mix mayonnaise and curry powder together. Add it to tuna mixture and blend well; chill. Just before serving, add walnuts. Serve on cabbage mixed with a little mayonnaise to moisten. Serves 6.

Picnic Potato Salad

Rhubarb 1 cup raw, finely diced
Tarragon wine vinegar 3 tablespoons
Dill seed 1 teaspoon
Mustard seed 1 teaspoon
Lemon juice 1 tablespoon
Honey 1 tablespoon
Salad oil 2 tablespoons
Prepared mustard 1 teaspoon
Capers 1 teaspoon
Salt 1 teaspoon
Garlic salt ½ teaspoon
Green onions with tops 3 tablespoons chopped
Parsley 3 tablespoons chopped
Cucumber ⅓, peeled and chopped
Coarse black pepper ½ teaspoon
Bacon slices 2, fried crisp and crumbled
Potatoes 3 cups cooked and diced

Cook rhubarb until barely tender with mixture of vinegar, dill and mustard seed, lemon juice, and honey. Cool slightly. Mix together oil, mustard, capers, salt, and garlic salt; add to rhubarb. Add rest of ingredients except pototoes; then pour over potatoes. Mix together carefully; chill to blend flavors. Serves 4.

Springtime Salad

Rhubarb 1 cup raw and finely diced
Orange juice 2 tablespoons
Honey ¼ cup
Ham 2 cups baked, cubed
Green beans 1 cup canned, drained
Celery ¾ cup finely diced
Onion ¼ cup minced
Walnuts ⅓ cup coarsely chopped
Mayonnaise ½ cup
Curry powder ½ teaspoon
Paprika ¼ teaspoon
Red wine vinegar 2 tablespoons
Salt to taste
Pepper to taste
Tomatoes 2, quartered
Green pepper 3 tablespoons minced

Simmer rhubarb in orange juice and honey until just tender, about 2 minutes; cool. Mix with ham, vegetables, and walnuts. Mix mayonnaise with seasonings and vinegar. Blend it into ham mixture, being careful not to mash up rhubarb; season. Garnish each plate with 2 tomato quarters and a sprinkling of green pepper. Serves 4.

Wonderful Waldorf

Rhubarb 1 cup finely diced
Beet juice coloring if needed*
Sugar ½ cup
Unflavored gelatin 1½ teaspoons
Orange juice ¼ cup
Cream cheese ½ of a 3-ounce package
Walnuts ⅓ cup chopped
Celery ⅔ cup finely diced
Raisins ¼ cup
Lemon juice 1 tablespoon
Lemon peel ½ teaspoon grated
Mayonnaise ¼ cup

Cook rhubarb, beet juice, and sugar together until just hot. Soften gelatin in orange juice; add to rhubarb mixture. Cut up cream cheese and stir into hot mixture; cook for 1 minute. Remove from heat and chill until it begins to thicken; stir in remaining ingredients. Pour into 2-cup fancy mold and chill; unmold to serve. Serves 4.
*This salad should be brightly colored to look its best.

One-Dish Six-Boy Curry Salad

Tuna   1 6½-ounce can, drained and flaked
Rice   2 cups cooked, cold
Celery   ½ cup diced
Green pepper   3 tablespoons minced
Onion   ¼ cup chopped
Raisins   ½ cup
Walnuts or peanuts   ¾ cup coarsely chopped
Shredded coconut   ¼ cup
Bacon bits or crumbled fried bacon   ¼ cup
Rhubarb sauce (see Index)   ½ cup sweetened
Mayonnaise   ½ cup
Salt   ½ teaspoon
Prepared mustard   ½ teaspoon
Garlic vinegar   1 tablespoon
Curry powder   1½ teaspoons (or more, according to taste)
Lemon juice   1 tablespoon

Mix first 9 ingredients together. Mix rhubarb sauce with remaining
ingredients; blend into salad. Chill to mix flavors. Serves 8.

Raw Rhubarb Royale

Cottage cheese 2 cups
Young red rhubarb stalks 1 cup raw and finely chopped
Carrots 1 cup coarsely grated
Green onions with tops ¼ cup chopped
Whole pitted black olives ½ cup
Radishes 3 tablespoons chopped
Oregano ¼ teaspoon crumbled
Mayonnaise ¼ cup
Salt to taste
Pepper to taste
Tomato 4 thick slices
Parsley sprigs 4

Mix first 8 ingredients together; season with salt and pepper. Mound salad on tomato slices or stuff tomatoes with the mixture; top with parsley. Serves 4.

Dilled Beet Salad

Beets 1 cup cooked, sliced, and quartered
Cucumber ½ cup sliced ¼-inch thick and quartered
Rhubarb sauce (see Index) ½ cup sweetened
Unflavored yogurt ¼ cup
Dillweed 1 teaspoon
Lemon juice 1 teaspoon
Salt to taste
Honey 1 tablespoon
Medium onion 3 center slices ⅛-inch thick, rings separated

Mix beets and cucumber. Mix together next 6 ingredients; pour over beet mixture and toss to coat. Mix in onion rings carefully and toss. Let chill for 1 hour or more. Serves 2 or 3.

Sweetly Sour Cukes

Cucumbers 2
Salt 1 teaspoon
Medium onion 1, peeled and thinly sliced in rings
Tarragon wine vinegar ¼ cup
Rhubarb sauce (see Index) ¼ cup slightly sweetened
Tomato 6 thick slices, peeled
Parsley 3 tablespoons minced

Peel cucumbers, run the tines of a fork down the sides all around (for a scalloped effect), and slice very thin. Salt them and let stand for a few minutes, stirring occasionally. Then drain and add onion. Mix vinegar and rhubarb together and pour over cucumber-onion mixture; chill. Serve on tomato slices; sprinkle with parsley. Serves 6.

Rhubarbarously Good Macaroni Salad

Macaroni 2½ cups cooked
Sharp cheddar cheese 1 cup small cubes
Pimiento ¼ cup chopped
Green onions with tops ¼ cup minced
Parsley 2 tablespoons minced
Green pepper ¼ cup finely chopped
Rhubarb sauce (see Index) 1 cup moderately sweetened and
   drained
Salt ½ teaspoon
Celery 1 cup diced
Tarragon vinegar 2 tablespoons
Mayonnaise ½ cup
Prepared mustard 1 teaspoon
Eggs 2 hard-cooked

Mix together all ingredients and chill well. Serves 6 to 8.

Pea Salad Confetti

Celery   ½ cup finely chopped
Eggs   2 hard-cooked and chopped
Onion   2 tablespoons minced
Prepared mustard   ½ teaspoon
Salt   ½ teaspoon
Dillweed   ½ teaspoon
Mayonnaise   ¼ cup
Rhubarb sauce (see Index)   ¼ cup sweetened and drained
Fresh or frozen peas   2 cups cooked until barely tender, drained
Tomato   1, peeled and cut into wedges

Mix together everything but the peas and tomato; blend well. Add to peas and stir gently to mix. Serve with tomato wedges. Serves 4.

Whipped Avocado Surprise

Large avocado   1
Lemon juice   2 tablespoons
Onion   2 tablespoons chopped
Garlic salt   ½ teaspoon
Tabasco   dash
Green pepper   2 tablespoons finely chopped
Unflavored yogurt   ½ cup
Large curd cottage cheese   1 cup
Mayonnaise   ⅓ cup
Rhubarb sauce (see Index)   ⅓ cup unsweetened and drained
Lettuce   shredded and crisp
Bacon slices   4, fried crisp and halved

Peel, seed, and mash avocado; add lemon juice. Add all other ingredients except bacon and lettuce, blending well. Serve on lettuce, with 2 halved bacon slices crisscrossed on each salad. Serves 4.

Dieters' Salad Dressing

Cottage cheese   1 cup
Unflavored yogurt   1 cup
Rhubarb sauce (see Index)   1 cup unsweetened
Egg   1
Mayonnaise   2 tablespoons
Honey   1 tablespoon
Tarragon vinegar   1 tablespoon
Garlic salt   ¼ teaspoon
Paprika   ⅛ teaspoon

Whirl all ingredients together in blender for a few seconds. Makes 3 cups.

Vegetables, Sauces, and Stuffings

Double Red Beets

Orange peel   1 teaspoon grated
Tarragon vinegar   2 tablespoons
Lemon juice   1 tablespoon
Margarine   2 tablespoons
Ginger   ⅛ teaspoon
Salt   ½ teaspoon
Rhubarb sauce (see Index)   ½ cup sweetened
Raisins   ¼ cup
Canned beets   2 cups sliced and drained
Cornstarch   1 teaspoon
Water or orange juice

Heat the first 8 ingredients together and simmer for a few minutes until raisins are plump. Add beets and simmer until beets are hot. If too thin, mix cornstarch with a little water and add, cooking until clear. Serves 4.

Be-Deviled Beets

Margarine   1 tablespoon, melted
Dry mustard   ½ teaspoon
Garlic vinegar   1 tablespoon
Orange juice   2 tablespoons
Honey   2 tablespoons
Salt   ½ teaspoon
Worcestershire sauce   2 teaspoons
Rhubarb sauce (see Index)   ½ cup slightly sweetened
Unflavored yogurt   3 tablespoons
Caraway seed   ½ teaspoon
Beets   2 cups cooked and sliced

Melt margarine. Mix mustard and vinegar together until smooth. Add remaining ingredients except for beets; simmer and stir to mix well. When hot, add beets and simmer until piping hot. Serves 4 to 6.

Braised Onions Deluxe

Onion   1 cup, sliced in rings
Green pepper   1, quartered and diced
Margarine   3 tablespoons, melted
Chicken broth or bouillon   ¾ cup
Brown sugar   3 tablespoons
Herb vinegar   1 to 2 tablespoons
Honey   2 tablespoons
Rhubarb sauce (see Index)   ¼ cup unsweetened
Cornstarch   1 teaspoon (optional)
Cold water   2 teaspoons

Sauté onions and green pepper in margarine until soft. Add chicken broth and simmer until onions are tender (5 to 10 minutes) and most of broth is absorbed. Then add remaining ingredients; simmer to glaze. If you want thicker sauce, mix cornstarch with cold water and stir in. Simmer until clear. Serves 4.

Note: This is an excellent side dish with meat.

Rhubi-Red Sweet-Sour Cabbage

Red cabbage   2 cups finely sliced
Margarine or bacon drippings   ¼ cup
Onion   ½ cup chopped
Rhubarb sauce (see Index)   1 cup unsweetened
Orange peel   ½ teaspoon grated
Brown sugar   3 tablespoons
Garlic vinegar   3 tablespoons
Mayonnaise   ⅓ cup
Caraway seeds   2 tablespoons

Fry cabbage in margarine until wilted. Add onion and fry for a few minutes. Add other ingredients and fry for 10 or 15 minutes over low heat. Serves 4.

Savory Pepper Fry

Large green peppers 3
Onion 1 cup sliced
Bacon fat 4 tablespoons
Garlic clove 1, minced
Rhubarb sauce (see Index) 3 tablespoons sweetened
Salt ¼ teaspoon
Red wine vinegar 2 teaspoons

Cut peppers in quarters; remove seeds and ribs. Place on a baking sheet under the broiler. Broil for about 5 to 10 minutes until blistered and dark. Scrape off skin with knife while peppers are hot. (Rebroil any part that does not peel.) Cut peppers lengthwise to make slices about ½-inch thick. Fry peppers and onions in bacon fat until onions are golden and peppers are limp (about 5 minutes). Add other ingredients and continue simmering for another five minutes. Serve with meat. Serves 4.

Festive Corn Fritters

Flour   1 cup sifted
Baking powder   1½ teaspoons
Salt   ¼ teaspoon
Sugar   1 teaspoon
Sage   ¼ teaspoon
Milk   ½ cup
Rhubarb sauce (see Index)   ½ cup unsweetened and drained
Egg yolk   1
Salad oil   1 tablespoon
Whole kernel canned corn   1 cup drained
Salad oil   ⅓ cup

Sift dry ingredients together. Combine milk, rhubarb, egg yolk, and 1 tablespoon of salad oil. Mix until smooth. Sift dry ingredients into rhubarb mixture. Blend only until moistened. Add corn and mix lightly. Drop in small cakes into hot oil. Fry 3 to 5 minutes until browned, turning once. Makes 8 fritters.

Creamy Cooked Cukes

Bacon slice   1
Margarine   2 tablespoons
Large cucumber   1, peeled, quartered lengthwise, sliced in chunks
Onion   2 tablespoons minced
Salt   ½ teaspoon
Mustard seed   ¼ teaspoon
Red wine garlic vinegar   ½ teaspoon
Dillweed   ½ teaspoon
Lemon juice   1 tablespoon
Rhubarb sauce (see Index)   ⅓ cup sweetened
Cream cheese   1 tablespoon
Mayonnaise   1 tablespoon
Cheddar cheese   3 tablespoons shredded

Fry bacon until crisp; remove from pan and crumble. In the fat and margarine, fry cucumber and onion for a few minutes. Add the next 5 ingredients and stir well; add rhubarb sauce. Simmer very gently until cucumbers are hot and tender but not soft. Stir in cream cheese, mayonnaise, and cheddar cheese, and simmer only until melted and hot. Serve at once, with bacon crumbled over each serving. Serves 4.

Nutty Sweet Potato Puffs

Sweet potatoes   3 cups boiled or baked and mashed
Margarine   ¼ cup
Honey or brown sugar   3 tablespoons
Lemon juice   1 tablespoon
Lemon peel   1 teaspoon grated
Bourbon   2 tablespoons (optional)
Salt   ½ teaspoon
Rhubarb sauce (see Index)   ½ cup unsweetened and drained
Pineapple chunks   12
Peanuts, walnuts, or pecans   1 cup finely chopped

Mash potatoes with margarine and honey. Blend in lemon juice and peel, bourbon, salt, and rhubarb sauce. Form into 12 small rolls or balls, enclosing a pineapple chunk in center of each. Roll each ball in nuts. Place on greased baking sheet. Bake for 15 minutes at 350°. Excellent with ham or turkey, and can be frozen. Serves 6.
Variation: Mix all ingredients together and spoon into greased 2-quart casserole. Bake 15 minutes at 375°. Sprinkle miniature marshmallows over the top and bake a few minutes longer until they are browned.

Sherried Zucchini Gourmand

Zucchini   1 ½ cups sliced in rounds ¼-inch thick
Margarine   3 tablespoons, melted
Green onions with tops   ½ cup chopped
Rhubarb   ½ cup finely diced
Sherry   2 tablespoons
Honey   2 tablespoons
Walnuts   ⅓ cup coarsely chopped

Sauté zucchini in margarine for a few minutes. Add onions and rhubarb; simmer and stir 5 minutes more. Add sherry and honey, and blend. Cover and simmer 5 minutes, shaking pan occasionally. Do not overcook. Add nuts just before serving. Serves 4.

Fancy Smothered Carrots

Carrots   1 cup cut in rounds ¼-inch thick
Orange juice   3 tablespoons
Orange peel   ¼ teaspoon grated
Ginger   ¼ teaspoon
Margarine   1 tablespoon
Honey   1 tablespoon
Rhubarb   ½ cup finely diced

Cook carrots in orange juice, with peel and ginger, until tender. Add margarine, honey, and rhubarb, and cook just 1 or 2 minutes until rhubarb is tender. Serves 3 to 4.

Holiday Sweet Potato Nests

Sweet potatoes or yams   3 cups cooked
Brown sugar   3 tablespoons
Margarine   3 tablespoons
Egg   1, beaten
Salt   ½ teaspoon
Pineapple slices   6
Brown sugar   ¼ cup
Dry mustard   1 teaspoon
Orange peel   ½ teaspoon grated
Cinnamon   ½ teaspoon
Cloves   ⅛ teaspoon
Tarragon vinegar   2 teaspoons
Rhubarb sauce (see Index)   ½ cup sweetened and drained
Raisins   ⅓ cup
Pecans or walnuts   6 halves

Mash the heated potatoes with sugar and margarine; let cool. Blend in egg and salt; divide into 6 parts. Put pineapple slices on a greased cookie sheet; mound some mixture on each slice, and form a nest in each center. Simmer the remaining ingredients together for a few minutes except for nuts. Fill nests with mixture. Top each with ½ a nut. Bake at 350° for 10 minutes. Serves 6.

Gilded Broccoli Amandine

Mayonnaise   ¼ cup
Rhubarb sauce (see Index)   2 tablespoons sweetened
Cheddar cheese   3 tablespoons grated
Pimiento   1 tablespoon finely chopped
Salt   1 teaspoon
Curry powder   ¼ to ½ teaspoon
Broccoli   1 pound cooked and drained, hot
Almonds   2 tablespoons blanched and slivered

Mix all ingredients but last 2 together and heat for a few minutes just until cheese melts. Pour over hot broccoli. Sprinkle with almonds. Serves 3 to 4.

Party Rice

Rice   1 cup
Chicken or turkey broth   2½ cups*
Salt   1 teaspoon
Onion   ¼ cup
Margarine   2 tablespoons, melted
Rhubarb sauce (see Index)   ⅓ cup slightly sweetened and drained
Walnuts or almonds   ⅓ cup chopped coarsely
Bacon   ¼ cup crisply fried and crumbled
Pitted black olives   ¼ cup sliced in thick rings
Cheddar or Swiss cheese   ⅓ cup shredded
Raisins   ¼ cup

Cook rice in broth with salt until rice is tender and broth is absorbed. Sauté onion in margarine until limp. Mix in other ingredients while rice is still hot. Or place them in separate bowls or divided dishes, and let guests add their own condiments to rice, as desired. Serves 4 to 6.
*If broth is from turkey carcass and has shreds of meat in it, so much the better. Just allow a bit more to make up for the displaced liquid.

Zesty Zucchini

Olive oil   2 tablespoons
Margarine   1 tablespoon, melted
Garlic clove   1, finely minced
Onion   ½ cup coarsely chopped
Zucchini   2 cups quartered and sliced ⅛-inch thick
Thyme   ¼ teaspoon
Salt   to taste
Pepper   to taste
Rhubarb sauce (see Index)   ⅓ cup slightly sweetened
Cheddar cheese   ½ cup shredded
Cracker crumbs   ¼ cup

Preheat oven to 350°. In the olive oil and margarine sauté garlic and onion until onion is soft. Add zucchini, thyme, salt, and pepper. Stir for a few minutes until zucchini is well coated but not soft. In individual casseroles, or in a 1-quart greased casserole, put ½ of the zucchini-onion mixture, spread with ½ of the rhubarb, and sprinkle ½ of the cheese on top. Repeat, ending with cheese. Sprinkle mixture with crumbs. Bake for about 10 minutes. Serves 4.

Pea and Carrot Caper

Margarine 3 tablespoons, melted
Onion ½ cup coarsely chopped
Rhubarb ⅔ cup finely diced
Carrots 1 cup cooked rounds
Fresh or frozen peas 1 cup cooked barely tender
Salt ½ teaspoon
Brown sugar 3 to 4 tablespoons
Coriander ½ teaspoon
Dry mustard ½ teaspoon
Prepared horseradish ½ to 1 teaspoon

In the melted margarine sauté onion and rhubarb until rhubarb is almost tender. Add carrots and peas. Stir together the remaining ingredients and sprinkle over mixture of vegetables. Cover and cook about 5 minutes more, shaking pan occasionally to mix. Makes about 4 servings.

Savory Seafood or Salad Sauce

Mayonnaise ¾ cup
Chili sauce 2 tablespoons
Rhubarb sauce (see Index) ½ cup unsweetened
Sharp cheddar cheese ⅓ cup shredded
Unflavored yogurt ½ cup
Olives ⅓ cup, cut in rings
Green onions with tops 2 tablespoons chopped
Capers 1 teaspoon

Mix all ingredients together. Makes about 2 cups.

Note: This is so delicious you won't even notice whether there is seafood in your Louis salad! The sauce may also be used as a sandwich spread.

Sauced Onions Dijon

Onion ½ cup minced
Drippings from steak skillet or roast pan 3 tablespoons
Dijon mustard 1 tablespoon
Garlic clove 1, minced
Rhubarb purée (see Index) ¼ cup unsweetened
Dry red wine 2 tablespoons
Worcestershire sauce 1 teaspoon

Sauté onion in skillet in which steak was fried, or in another skillet to which drippings have been transferred. Gradually mix in other ingredients; simmer until well blended. Pour over steak (which has been kept hot in oven). Enough for 4 servings.

Avocado Nectar

Large avocado 1, peeled and seeded
Unflavored yogurt ½ cup
Rhubarb sauce (see Index) ¼ cup slightly sweetened
Lemon juice 1 tablespoon
Soy sauce 2 teaspoons
Honey 1 tablespoon
Salt ¼ teaspoon

Put all ingredients into blender and whirl for a few seconds until well mixed. Makes about 1¼ cups.

Note: This is delectable on fruit salads, fruit compotes, or melon balls.

Zesty Meat Sauce

Prepared horseradish   1 teaspoon
Lemon juice   2 teaspoons
Lemon peel   1 teaspoon grated
Prepared mustard   1 teaspoon
Rhubarb sauce (see Index)   1 cup slightly sweetened
Mayonnaise   ¾ cup

Mix all ingredients together. Serve with chicken, boiled beef, bockwurst, or stew. Makes 2 cups.

Continental Caper

Margarine   1 tablespoon
Flour   1 tablespoon
Chicken broth or bouillon   ¼ cup
Rhubarb sauce (see Index)   2 tablespoons slightly sweetened
Lemon juice   2 teaspoons
Capers   2 teaspoons drained
Caper liquid   1 teaspoon
Tarragon vinegar   1 tablespoon
Salt   to taste
Pepper   to taste

Melt margarine, stir in flour, and blend in broth. Add rhubarb sauce and other ingredients. Simmer a few minutes until smooth and slightly thick; add water if sauce is too thick. Serve over meat. Makes about ½ cup.

Three Savory Ham Sauces

1. **Rhubarb sauce** (see Index) ¼ cup unsweetened
   Honey or brown sugar ⅓ cup
   Prepared mustard 2 tablespoons

   Mix all ingredients together.

2. **Rhubarb sauce** (see Index) 2 cups unsweetened
   Brown sugar ½ cup
   Catsup ¼ cup
   Vinegar ¼ cup
   Soy sauce 2 tablespoons
   Garlic clove 1, minced
   Ginger 1 teaspoon
   Salt 1 teaspoon
   Chili powder 1 teaspoon
   Worcestershire sauce 2 tablespoons

   Mix all ingredients together.

3. **Rhubarb sauce** (see Index) 1 cup unsweetened
   Curry powder ¼ teaspoon
   Prepared horseradish 1 teaspoon
   Brown sugar ⅓ cup
   Orange juice enough to thin to desired consistency

   Mix all ingredients together.

Note: These 3 sauces can be spread on a 1- or 2-inch thick slice of ham, with its edges slashed to prevent curling. Bake covered in greased shallow baking dish at 350° for 20 minutes; bake uncovered for 30 minutes. Serves 2 to 4. These sauces are also excellent on pork spareribs or as a glaze on a baking ham.

Toasty Cheese Stuffing

Whole wheat bread   2 cups 1-inch cubes, lightly toasted
Tender rhubarb stalks   ½ cup finely diced
Sharp cheddar cheese   ½ cup
Walnuts   2 tablespoons chopped
Onion   2 tablespoons chopped
Margarine   2 tablespoons, melted
Honey   2 tablespoons
Dry white wine or orange juice   2 tablespoons
Salt   ¼ teaspoon
Tarragon   ¼ teaspoon crumbled

Lightly mix first 5 ingredients. Then mix together last 5 ingredients and drizzle over bread mixture; toss lightly. Use between ham slices or as a stuffing for pork chops. Or bake as a side dish in a greased 8-inch square pan for 15 minutes until toasty and hot. Serves 4.

Fruited Pilaf Stuffing

Margarine or bacon fat ⅓ cup
Onion 1 cup chopped
Green pepper 1 quarter, chopped
Celery and leaves 1 cup chopped
Uncooked brown rice 1 cup
Salt 1 teaspoon
Chicken broth 3 cups hot
Rhubarb 1½ cups finely diced
Raisins ½ cup
Sherry ¼ cup
Whole wheat bread 3 cups slightly stale and coarsely shredded
Almonds ½ cup chopped
Ginger ¼ teaspoon
Cinnamon ½ teaspoon
Lemon peel 1 teaspoon grated

Melt margarine in a large, heavy skillet. Sauté onion, green pepper, and celery until soft. Add rice and sauté 5 minutes more. Add salt and 2¾ cups of chicken broth. Cover and simmer until rice is tender (35 to 40 minutes); most of the liquid will be absorbed; stir occasionally. Add rhubarb, raisins, and sherry. Simmer for about 5 minutes until rhubarb is slightly soft. Combine bread, nuts, spices, and lemon peel. Add to rice mixture and blend well; let cool slightly. Then test for moistness by squeezing a handful together; it should just hold together. If too dry, add the additional broth. If too moist, add more bread. Excellent stuffing for fowl, ham, or pork.

Variation: To make stuffing balls, add a beaten egg to the stuffing so it holds together better. Dip each 2-inch ball in a mixture of 1 cup of dry bread crumbs, ¼ cup toasted sesame seeds, and ¼ cup margarine. Bake in a well-greased 9 by 13-inch shallow pan at 325° for 30 minutes or until crusty.

Relishes and Jams

Savory Catsup

Rhubarb   4 cups diced
Cinnamon   1 tablespoon
Cloves   1 teaspoon
Allspice   1 teaspoon
Sugar   2½ cups
Vinegar   1 cup
Cayenne   sprinkle

Simmer all together until thick (about 1 hour). Seal in hot sterilized jars. Process in boiling water bath for 10 minutes. Makes 4 cups.

Mustardy Meat Relish

Medium onion   1, sliced in ¼-inch rings
Rhubarb   ½ cup chopped 1-inch thick
Mustard seed   1 teaspoon
Cider vinegar   ½ cup
Prepared mustard   1 teaspoon
Honey   2 tablespoons
Celery   ½ cup chopped

Cover and simmer onion, rhubarb, and mustard seed in vinegar until barely tender (about 5 minutes). Mix mustard and honey and add carefully to relish. Add celery and cover pan; let stand until cool. Serve on chops or roasts. Makes about 1½ cups.

Instant Meat Relish

Rhubarb sauce (see Index)   ¾ cup sweetened and drained
Sweet hamburger relish   ¼ cup, drained
Raisins   ¼ cup
Curry powder   ½ teaspoon

Mix together all ingredients. Serve with any meat. Makes 1¼ cups.

Scandinavian Relish au Vin

Water   ⅓ cup
Sugar or honey   ⅓ cup
Lemon   2 1-inch thick slices
Whole cloves   3
Cinnamon   ¼ teaspoon
Ginger root   2 thin slices
Dry red wine   ½ cup
Rhubarb   2 cups diced 1-inch thick
Cornstarch   1 teaspoon
Cold water   2 teaspoons

Simmer together everything but last 4 ingredients for 10 minutes. Add wine and heat to a simmer. Add rhubarb, turn off heat at once, and cover pan. Let cool. Remove ginger, lemon slices, and cloves; chill. This sauce can be thickened by draining off juice and heating it with cornstarch mixed with cold water; simmer until clear. Add rhubarb again, being careful not to mash it up. Makes 2 cups.

New Zealand Rhubarb Chutney

Rhubarb   3 cups diced in 1-inch pieces
Cider vinegar   1 cup
Onion   2 cups thinly sliced
Garlic clove   1, minced
Curry powder   2 teaspoons
Brown sugar   1½ cups
Salt   1 teaspoon
Cloves   ½ teaspoon
Cayenne   ⅛ teaspoon
Cinnamon   1 teaspoon
Ginger root   1 tablespoon grated
Lemon   1, grated peel, juice, and pulp
Raisins   ½ cup
Prepared mustard   1½ teaspoons
Mustard seeds   2 tablespoons

Simmer all ingredients together over low heat, stirring occasionally,
until thick (about 30 to 40 minutes). Pack into sterilized ½-pint jars
and process 10 minutes in boiling water bath. Makes about 3 pints.

Note: This keeps unsealed in refrigerator for several months.

Burgundy-Barb

Crushed pineapple   2 cups drained
Rhubarb   8 cups coarsely sliced
Ginger   2 teaspoons
Sugar   3½ cups
Dry red wine   1 cup

Mix all together in large kettle. Stir well and cook at a slow boil for about 30 minutes. Test for thickness by dropping a little on a saucer and letting it cool. Seal with paraffin in hot sterilized jars. Makes 8 cups.

Berry Good Jam

Fresh or frozen blueberries   2 cups
Rhubarb   3 cups diced
Lemon juice   2 tablespoons
Sugar   5 cups

Crush berries; add rhubarb and lemon juice; mix in sugar. Bring to boil over a slow fire, stirring occasionally. Simmer until a little of the jam placed on a saucer is thick enough. Seal with paraffin in hot sterilized glasses or in canning jars. Makes about 4 cups.

Raspbarby Jam

Rhubarb   3 cups finely chopped
Fresh or frozen raspberries   1 cup
Tart apple sauce   1 cup unsweetened
Sugar   4 cups

Combine fruit; stir in sugar; cook at a slow boil for about 30 minutes. Test for thickness by dropping a little on a saucer. Seal in hot sterilized jars with paraffin or canning lids. Makes about 4 cups.

Jean's Jam Superbe

Rhubarb   5 cups finely diced
Sugar   4 cups
Strawberry Jell-O   1 3-ounce package
Walnuts   1 cup chopped
Ginger root   1 tablespoon finely chopped
Candied fruit   ½ cup (optional)

Cover rhubarb with sugar and let stand for 1 hour or more, stirring occasionally. Cook slowly until tender (about 10 minutes). Remove from heat and stir in Jell-O. Add walnuts, ginger root, and candied fruit. Seal with paraffin. Delicious over ice cream or pudding. Makes about 6 cups.

Glorified Rhubi Conserve

Rhubarb   1½ cups diced
Raisins   ½ cup
Sugar   1½ cups
Orange   1, grated peel, juice, and pulp
Lemon   ½, grated peel, juice, and pulp
Ginger root   1½ tablespoons peeled and finely chopped
Large strawberries   2 cups sliced
Walnuts   ½ cup chopped or halved

Mix together rhubarb, raisins, sugar, orange, lemon, and ginger root. Let stand at least 1 hour, stirring occasionally. Bring rhubarb mixture to a boil. Add berries and bring to a boil again; simmer for 25 minutes. Add nuts the last 5 minutes. Seal with paraffin in sterilized jars or in ½-pint canning jars in boiling water bath for 10 minutes. Serve over French toast or pancakes. Makes 3 cups.

Piquant Pepper Jam

Rhubarb   1 cup finely diced
Sugar   1 cup
Large green pepper   1
Salt   ½ teaspoon
Tarragon vinegar   ¼ cup

Mix rhubarb and sugar and let stand for about 1 hour. Grind green pepper through fine blade. Add salt and let stand until rhubarb is ready; drain and discard pepper juice. Mix rhubarb and pepper with vinegar and simmer gently for about 30 minutes. Makes about 1½ cups of jam-relish for meats.

Marmalade Hawaiiana

Rhubarb   3 cups diced
Sugar   2 cups
Crushed pineapple   ½ cup
Small orange   1, grated peel, juice, and pulp
Lemon   ½, grated peel, juice, and pulp
Ginger root   1 small knob, grated

Let rhubarb stand in sugar for several hours or overnight. Add rest of ingredients. Bring to a boil and simmer for about 30 minutes until thick. Seal in jars with canning lids or paraffin. Makes 3 cups.

Winey Rhubarb Jelly-Jam

Rhubarb   4 cups finely diced
Sugar   4½ cups
Dry red wine   1 cup
Lemon juice   1 tablespoon
Liquid pectin   ½ bottle

Soak rhubarb in 3 cups of sugar for 1 hour or overnight. Then simmer gently until sugar dissolves and rhubarb is barely tender (about 5 minutes). Add rest of sugar, wine, and lemon juice and bring to a good boil. Remove from heat and stir in pectin. Pour into hot sterilized glasses or canning jars; seal with paraffin or canning lids. Makes 6 8-ounce glasses.

Main Dishes

Beef Broil Dijon

Ground beef   1 pound
Egg   1, slightly beaten
Soft bread crumbs   1 cup
Onion   3 tablespoons minced
Celery   ¼ cup minced
Dijon mustard   1 teaspoon
Salt   1 teaspoon
Rhubarb sauce (see Index)   ½ cup unsweetened
Brown sugar   3 tablespoons
Red wine vinegar   1 tablespoon
Rhubarb sauce (see Index)   ½ cup unsweetened
Dijon mustard   1 teaspoon

Preheat oven to 350°. Mix together first 8 ingredients. Form 6 patties, cupping up edges to hold a sauce; put them in a heavy pan that can withstand broiling. Combine last 4 ingredients, and pour into center of patties. Bake for about 20 minutes. Then put under broiler for a few minutes to brown. Serves 6.

Sauerbarb Patties

Ground beef   1 pound
Egg   1, slightly beaten
Onion   ⅓ cup finely chopped
Dry bread crumbs   ¼ cup
Salt   1 teaspoon
Prepared mustard   1 tablespoon
Water   1 cup
Gingersnap crumbs   ½ cup
Brown sugar   2 tablespoons
Raisins   2 tablespoons
Lemon juice   2 tablespoons
Rhubarb sauce (see Index)   ⅓ cup unsweetened
Beef bouillon cube   1

Mix first 6 ingredients together; make 8 patties. Brown them well in a large skillet, turning once; drain off excess fat. Mix together remaining ingredients. Pour over meat patties. Cover skillet and simmer for 15 to 20 minutes. Stir occasionally. If it gets too thick, add a little water. Serves 8.

Sweet-Sour Rhuburger Balls

Ground beef   1 pound
Egg   1, beaten
Onion   ¼ cup chopped
Water chestnuts or Jerusalem artichokes   ¼ cup chopped
Cornstarch   ¼ cup
Salt   ½ teaspoon
Soy sauce   ¼ cup
Cooking oil   ½ cup
Sherry   2 tablespoons
Rhubarb sauce (see Index)   2 cups sweetened with honey
Chicken bouillon   ½ cup

Combine beef, egg, onion, water chestnuts, 2 tablespoons corn-starch, salt, and 2 tablespoons soy sauce. Form into 20 2-inch balls; fry them in a heavy skillet in the oil; drain. Put 1 tablespoon of oil in skillet; add sherry, rhubarb, and chicken bouillon. Add remaining 2 tablespoons soy sauce mixed with remaining 2 tablespoons corn-starch. Let cook until bubbling and thickened. Add the meat balls and heat well. Serve in 4 individual bowls or as an appetizer, with toothpicks, in a chafing dish.

Chilean Corn-Meat Pie

Large onions 2, chopped
Margarine 3 tablespoons
Very lean beef 1 pound coarsely chopped
Raisins ⅓ cup
Parsley ¼ cup chopped
Cumin ½ teaspoon
Paprika ¼ teaspoon
Salt to taste
Rhubarb sauce (see Index) ½ cup sweetened and drained
Eggs 2 hard-cooked, sliced
Pitted black olives ½ cup
Cooked chicken or turkey 4 medium-thick slices
Creamed corn 3 cups
Margarine 3 tablespoons
Sugar 2 tablespoons
Flour ¼ cup

Preheat oven to 350°. Sauté onions in margarine until soft. Add beef, raisins, parsley, and seasonings. Cook until meat is done. Spread meat in bottom of 1½-quart buttered casserole. Spread on a thin layer of rhubarb sauce; top with slices of egg, olives, and then the slices of chicken. Heat corn in skillet with remaining ingredients. Adjust sugar to your taste. The Chileans like it rather sweet. Pour the cooked corn topping over the meat. Bake for about 15 minutes until topping is browned and all is piping hot. Also good in individual casseroles. Serves 6 to 8.

Tart Layered Burgers

Ground beef   1 pound
Egg   1, beaten
Dry onion soup mix   1 package
Salt   ½ teaspoon
Worcestershire sauce   1 tablespoon
Carrots   2 cups sliced and cooked
Rhubarb sauce (see Index)   1 cup slightly sweetened and drained
Onion   ½ cup sliced

Preheat oven to 350°. Mix beef with egg, soup mix, salt, and Worcestershire sauce. Divide into 8 parts and form patties. Lay 4 patties in a greased 9 by 13-inch baking pan. Spread them with carrots, rhubarb sauce, and onion. Top with another patty and seal the edges with a fork. Bake for 30 minutes. Serves 4.

Rhubarbeque Stew

Flour ¼ cup
Cinnamon ¼ teaspoon
Pepper ⅛ teaspoon
Ginger ⅛ teaspoon
Salt 1 teaspoon
Beef stew meat 1 pound
Cooking oil 3 tablespoons
Onion ½ cup sliced
Catsup ½ cup
Vinegar ⅓ cup
Brown sugar 2 tablespoons
Prepared mustard 2 teaspoons
Salt ½ teaspoon
Rhubarb sauce (see Index) 1 cup unsweetened
Vegetables carrots, potatoes, peas, or others

Mix flour and seasonings in a plastic bag; add well-trimmed stew
pieces, cut smaller if desired; shake well to coat. Brown in oil in
pressure cooker until crusty. Add onion and sauté for a few minutes.
Add other ingredients except for vegetables. Cook under pressure
for 12 minutes; add prepared vegetables and cook another 5 minutes
under pressure. Serves 4.

Spiced Beef Special

Chuck pot roast or beef round steak 2 pounds
Flour seasoned with salt, pepper, paprika ⅓ cup
Cooking oil 4 tablespoons
Onion ½ cup coarsely chopped
Beef bouillon 1 cup
Dry red wine ½ cup
Lemon juice 2 tablespoons
Rhubarb sauce (see Index) 1 cup sweetened
Ginger ½ teaspoon
Marjoram ½ teaspoon
Carrots 1½ cups thickly sliced
Cornstarch 1 tablespoon
Water or orange juice ¼ cup

Pound roast with seasoned flour on all sides. Or cut steak into 6
serving pieces, and shake with flour in bag. Brown in pressure
cooker in oil, adding onion just before done. Add bouillon, wine, and
lemon juice, and cook under pressure for ½ hour or until tender;
release pressure; add rhubarb sauce, spices, and carrots. Cook without pressure for another 15 minutes until carrots are tender. Mix
cornstarch with water and add to cooking liquid to thicken to
desired consistency. Serves 6.

Bon Vivant Meatballs

Ground beef 1 pound
Rhubarb sauce (see Index) 1 cup sweetened with honey and drained
Eggs 2, beaten slightly
Wheat germ ½ cup
Dry bread crumbs ½ cup
Onion ¼ cup minced
Green pepper ¼ cup minced
Salt 1 teaspoon
Sage ½ teaspoon
Cream of celery soup 1 10½-ounce can
Tomato juice 1 cup
Rice or noodles cooked

Preheat oven to 350°. Mix together all but the soup, juice, and rice. Form into 2-inch balls. Place in a greased 1-quart casserole and pour the soup, diluted with tomato juice, over them. Bake covered for 45 minutes; uncover and bake another 10 minutes. Serve on rice. Serves 4.

Sherried Onion Skillet Supper

Large onions   4, sliced into ½-inch rounds
Beef or chicken bouillon   ½ cup
Fresh mushrooms   1 cup sliced
Rhubarb sauce (see Index)   1 cup moderately sweet
Sherry   2 tablespoons
Sausage   1 pound, shaped into 4 patties
Sharp cheddar cheese   ⅔ cup shredded
Walnuts   ½ cup coarsely chopped

Put onions into a large skillet. Pour bouillon over them and cover pan; simmer for about 5 minutes. Add mushrooms and rhubarb sauce; sprinkle with sherry; then simmer for another 5 minutes. In another skillet, fry sausage patties until done, pouring off grease as it accumulates. Lay patties on top of onion mixture. Sprinkle with cheese and top with walnuts. Heat till piping hot (about 5 minutes) in a 350° oven. Serves 4.

Sherried Ham 'n' Sweets

Orange juice   ¾ cup
Sherry   ½ cup
Brown sugar   ¾ cup
Prepared mustard   1 tablespoon
Cloves   ⅛ teaspoon
Orange peel   2 teaspoons grated
Rhubarb sauce (see Index)   ½ cup sweetened
Ham   2 1-inch thick slices
Sweet potatoes   3 pounds canned or cooked, peeled and sliced

Mix first 7 ingredients together and simmer for a few minutes to dissolve sugar. Marinate ham slices in this sauce for several hours in refrigerator. Place 1 slice in greased 9 by 13-inch baking pan and pour ½ of sauce over it. Top with sweet potatoes and other ham slice, and pour remaining sauce over it. Bake at 325° for about 45 minutes, basting occasionally. Serves 6 to 8.

Ginger Crumbled Ham

Rhubarb sauce (see Index)   1½ cups sweetened
Gingersnap cookie crumbs   1 cup*
Lemon juice   2 teaspoons
Cinnamon   ¼ teaspoon
Lemon peel   ½ teaspoon grated
Canned ham   3 to 5 pounds or 2-inch thick center slice

Preheat oven to 350°. Mix together everything but ham. Spread sauce over ham. Bake in a greased shallow pan for 1½ hours (or 45 minutes if you use center slice); baste occasionally.
*Any cookie crumbs, including graham cracker crumbs, can be used; just add ½ teaspoon ground ginger to give spiciness.

Curried Pork Supreme

Margarine or bacon fat   3 tablespoons
Garlic clove   1, minced
Pork roast or steaks   1 pound cut in cubes
Cream of mushroom soup   1 10½-ounce can
Unflavored yogurt   ½ cup
Green pepper   2 tablespoons chopped
Green onions with tops   3 tablespoons chopped
Curry powder   1 teaspoon
Soy sauce   1 teaspoon
Rhubarb sauce (see Index)   1 cup slightly sweetened
Rice   hot

Heat margarine and sauté garlic and meat cubes in it until meat is browned. Add remaining ingredients except rice and mix well. Cover and simmer for 30 minutes until meat is tender. Serve over hot rice. Serves 6.

Pork Chops Epicurean

Pork chops 4, with fat trimmed off
Cooking oil 2 tablespoons
Salt 1 teaspoon
Marjoram 1 teaspoon dried
Dry mustard 1 teaspoon
Orange peel 1 teaspoon grated
Worcestershire sauce ½ teaspoon
Rhubarb sauce (see Index) ½ cup unsweetened
Raisins ¼ cup
Brown sugar 2 tablespoons
Orange juice or dry white wine ½ cup
Flour 2 tablespoons
Cold water
Orange 1, peeled and cut into segments

Brown chops well in oil. Mix together salt, marjoram, mustard, and orange peel; rub into meat on both sides with back of a spoon. Mix together Worcestershire sauce, rhubarb, raisins, brown sugar, and orange juice; pour it around chops and let simmer covered for about 20 minutes, basting occasionally. Remove meat from skillet and keep it warm in oven. Thicken sauce with flour mixed with a little cold water. Return chops to skillet until they are piping hot. Top with orange segments. Serves 4.

Devilishly Delicious Lamb Steaks

Lamb shoulder chops   4
Cooking oil   3 tablespoons
Garlic salt   1 teaspoon
Rhubarb   1¼ cups finely diced
Orange juice   ½ cup
Dry red wine   ¼ cup
Honey   1 tablespoon
Chicken bouillon cube   1, crushed
Prepared mustard   ¼ cup
Oregano   ½ teaspoon
Onion   4 ¼-inch thick slices
Green pepper   4 ¼-inch thick rings
Lemon   4 slices, seeded and thinly cut
Mustard seed   1 teaspoon
Cheddar cheese   ¼ cup grated

Brown both sides of chops in oil; sprinkle each side with garlic salt. Simmer rhubarb in mixture of orange juice, wine, honey, and bouillon for 5 minutes. When chops are browned, spread 1 side of each with mixture of mustard and oregano. Place an onion slice, a green pepper ring, and a lemon slice on each; sprinkle mustard seed over all. Simmer covered for about 25 minutes, basting occasionally. Sprinkle cheese on each chop and simmer, covered, 5 minutes or more. Serve with rhubarb sauce. Serves 4.

Lamb Piquant

Lamb shoulder roast   3 pounds, cubed to make 4 cups
Margarine   2 tablespoons
Onion   ¼ cup chopped
Garlic clove   1, minced
Green pepper   2 tablespoons chopped
Flour   1 tablespoon
Chicken broth   1 cup
Coconut milk (see Index)   ½ cup
Rhubarb   1½ cups finely diced
Curry powder   1½ teaspoons
Raisins   ½ cup
Lemon juice   1 tablespoon
Rice   cooked
Condiments   chopped peanuts, coconut, crisp bacon*

Brown lamb cubes in margarine. Add onion, garlic, and green pepper and sauté until golden; stir in flour. Then add broth and coconut milk. When smooth, blend in rest of ingredients except for hot rice and condiments. Simmer for 45 minutes until tender, adding more broth as needed. Serve on hot rice. Pass condiments as desired. Serves 3 to 4.
*You can use other condiments of your choice.

Deviled Chicken

Margarine ½ cup
Honey ½ cup
Prepared mustard ⅓ cup
Rhubarb purée (see Index) 1 cup sweetened
Water ½ cup
Ginger ½ teaspoon
Curry powder 1 teaspoon
Frying chicken 2½ pounds, cut in serving pieces with skin removed
Salt to taste

Preheat oven to 300°. In a large heavy skillet, mix together all ingredients but chicken and salt. Stir over low heat until margarine is melted. Add chicken and coat pieces with sauce. Turn them meaty side up and salt lightly. Bake for 45 minutes, basting every 15 minutes and turning legs and thighs. If sauce becomes too thick, add a little more water. Serves 4.

Ground Turkey Gustoso

Ground turkey   1 pound
Mushrooms   1 cup minced
Onion   3 tablespoons minced
Celery   4 tablespoons finely chopped
Curry powder   ½ teaspoon
Sage   1 teaspoon
Salt   ½ teaspoon
Black pepper   ¼ teaspoon
Margarine   3 tablespoons, melted
Rhubarb sauce (see Index)   ½ cup unsweetened
Cornstarch   1 tablespoon
Dry white wine   3 tablespoons
Cream of chicken soup   1 10½-ounce can
Biscuit dough   2-cup recipe

Preheat oven to 400°. Mix first 8 ingredients. Fry in margarine for a few minutes until meat loses raw look. Stir in rhubarb sauce. Mix the cornstarch blended with wine into ⅓ of the soup. Stir this soup mixture into meat mixture and let it heat through. Turn this mixture into a 1½-quart greased casserole or into 6 individual greased ramekins. Top with biscuit dough rolled out to fit. Bake for 12 to 15 minutes. Serve with the rest of the heated soup poured over; dilute it with a little milk or wine if desired. Serves 6.

Fred's Fruity Fowl

Flour ½ cup
Salt 1 teaspoon
Celery salt ¼ teaspoon
Garlic salt ¼ teaspoon
Paprika ¼ teaspoon
Broiler-fryer chicken 1, cut in serving pieces
Cooking oil 4 tablespoons
Rhubarb sauce (see Index) 1 cup unsweetened
Honey ¼ cup
Tarragon vinegar 3 tablespoons
Dry mustard ½ teaspoon
Soy sauce ⅓ cup
Orange juice 1 cup
Walnuts 1 cup chopped

Mix first 5 ingredients in plastic bag. Shake chicken pieces in bag until well coated; fry in oil in heavy skillet until browned. Mix together other ingredients except for nuts; pour over chicken. Cover and cook on top of stove for 40 minutes over low heat, turning and basting several times, or bake in 350° oven for 45 minutes or more, basting occasionally. Sauce can also be used as a marinade for chicken to be barbecued and as a basting sauce. To serve, sprinkle nuts over chicken on serving plate. Serves 4.

Tart 'n' Spicy Turkey Legs

Turkey legs 2 or
Lamb shanks 4
Flour ¼ cup
Salt 1 teaspoon
Pepper ¼ teaspoon
Ginger ¼ teaspoon
Paprika 1 teaspoon
Cloves ¼ teaspoon
Cooking oil 3 tablespoons
Onion ½ cup chopped
Garlic clove 1 minced or pressed
Orange peel 1 teaspoon grated
Rhubarb sauce (see Index) 1 cup unsweetened
Orange juice 3 tablespoons
Parsley 1 teaspoon minced
Tomato soup 1 10½-ounce can diluted with 1 cup water
Cornstarch 2 teaspoons
Cold water
Rice cooked

Put turkey legs into a paper bag with flour and spices; shake until well coated. Heat oil in pressure cooker and brown meat well. Sauté onion and garlic after meat is browned. Add next 5 ingredients. Cook under pressure for 45 minutes (or cook slowly on top of stove for 2 to 2½ hours). If sauce is too thin, remove meat and thicken sauce with cornstarch mixed with water. Cut meat off bone; serve over hot rice. Serves 4.

Burgundy-Barb Chicken

Frying chicken 2½ pounds, cut in serving pieces
Flour seasoned with salt, pepper, paprika ½ cup
Margarine 4 tablespoons, melted
Onion ½ cup chopped
Garlic clove 1, minced
Rhubarb sauce (see Index) 1 cup sweetened
Burgundy wine 1 cup
Thyme ½ teaspoon
Oregano ½ teaspoon
Salt to taste
Lemon 1, thinly sliced

Shake chicken pieces in seasoned flour until well coated; brown
them well in margarine in heavy skillet; keep warm in oven while you
prepare the sauce. Sauté onion until soft in chicken drippings. Add
garlic, rhubarb, wine, and seasonings; simmer for a few minutes.
Return chicken to skillet; lightly salt each piece, and lay lemon
slices on the top. Bake at 350° for about 1 hour; baste occasionally.
Serves 4.

Wine-Curried Chicken Breasts

Chicken breasts   3, split in half and boned
Margarine   ¼ cup
Salt   ½ teaspoon
Onion   ½ cup chopped
Garlic clove   1, minced
Rhubarb   1½ cups finely diced
Chicken broth   1 cup
Dry white wine   ½ cup
Coconut milk (see Index)   ½ cup
Flour   2 tablespoons
Curry powder   1 to 2 teaspoons
Dry mustard   1 teaspoon
Ginger   ½ teaspoon
Honey   2 tablespoons

Sauté chicken breasts in margarine and salt until quite well done; remove from pan and keep warm. Sauté onion and garlic, adding rhubarb after onion is soft; sauté until rhubarb is fairly soft. Mix 3 liquids together. Mix flour and seasonings; stir into rhubarb mixture. Gradually add liquid, stirring, and simmer until thick and smooth. Add honey and blend well. Return chicken to pan and continue to simmer for about 20 minutes until chicken is well cooked and hot. If sauce gets too thick, add more chicken broth. Serves 6.

Halibut Hullabaloo

Halibut steak or turbot fillets   2 pounds
Rhubarb purée (see Index)   1 cup unsweetened
Dry red wine   ¼ cup
Cornstarch   1 tablespoon
Salad oil   2 tablespoons
Salt   1 teaspoon
Green onions with tops   3 tablespoons chopped
Tarragon   ½ teaspoon crumbled
Chicken bouillon cube   1
Mushrooms   ½ cup chopped
Parsley sprigs   3, chopped

Preheat oven to 350°. Lay fish in a greased shallow 9 by 13-inch pan. Mix together all other ingredients but parsley, and simmer for a few minutes until thick. Pour over fish. Bake for 20 minutes, basting a few times. Sprinkle fish with parsley and serve. Serves 6.

Shrimp Baiana

Milk ¾ cup
Flaked coconut 1½ cups
Oil of dende* or peanut oil 2 tablespoons
Margarine 2 tablespoons, melted
Onion 1 cup chopped
Garlic clove 1, minced
Rhubarb 1 cup finely diced
Green pepper ½ cup coarsely chopped
Shrimp 1 pound raw, peeled, and deveined
Fresh tomatoes 2, chopped
Coconut milk
Salt ½ teaspoon
Cornstarch 1 teaspoon
Cold water 2 teaspoons
Rice 3 to 4 cups cooked

Heat milk and let coconut stand in it for at least 1 hour. Using a piece of cheesecloth, wring milk from coconut; discard coconut. In oil and margarine, sauté onion, garlic, rhubarb, and green pepper for about 5 minutes until onion is soft. Add shrimp and tomatoes and sauté for another 5 minutes; add coconut milk and salt. Let simmer until piping hot. If it needs thickening, add cornstarch dissolved in cold water. Serve on hot rice. Serves 4.

*This is a bright red yellow oil from Brazil that adds a delectable flavor and color. You may be able to purchase it in a food speciality store.

Flavory Stuffed Fillets

Celery ⅓ cup finely chopped
Onion ¼ cup chopped
Margarine 3 tablespoons
Stale bread cubes 2 cups
Lemon peel ½ teaspoon grated
Lemon juice 1 teaspoon
Parsley 1 tablespoon minced
Salt ½ teaspoon
Tarragon ½ teaspoon crumbled
Rhubarb sauce (see Index) ⅓ cup slightly sweetened and drained
Fish fillets 2 pounds
Salt to taste
Margarine 1 tablespoon, melted
Salt to taste
Pepper to taste
Paprika to taste

Preheat oven to 350°. Sauté celery and onion in 3 tablespoons margarine until just tender. Add next 7 ingredients; stir to blend. In a greased 8-inch square baking pan, lay 1 pound of fish fillet (thawed if frozen). Salt it, and cover with stuffing. Lay other fillet on top. Drizzle 1 tablespoon margarine over fish, and season with salt, pepper, and paprika. Cover pan with foil and bake for 20 minutes. Uncover and bake for 5 minutes longer. Serves 4 to 6.

Cantonese Cucumber Shrimp

Raw large shrimp or prawns   1 pound, peeled and deveined
Margarine   4 tablespoons, melted
Green onions with tops   3 tablespoons
Green pepper   3 tablespoons coarsely chopped
Red wine vinegar   2 tablespoons
Lemon juice   1 tablespoon
Soy sauce   1 tablespoon
Lemon peel   1 teaspoon grated
Rhubarb sauce (see Index)   ½ cup moderately sweet
Fresh ginger root   1 tablespoon finely chopped
Cornstarch   2 teaspoons
Chicken broth   ¼ cup
Cucumber   1, peeled and cut in bite-size chunks
Rice   cooked

Sauté shrimp in margarine in heavy skillet. Remove shrimp and sauté onions and green pepper. Mix vinegar, lemon juice, soy sauce, lemon peel, rhubarb, and ginger root, and add to skillet. Return shrimp to skillet and simmer gently. Mix cornstarch in cold chicken broth and add to skillet; add cucumber and simmer for a few minutes until sauce is thick and bubbling hot. Serve on rice or in individual serving bowls. Serves 4.

Louisiana Dinner Eggs

Bacon slices   4, fried crisp and crumbled
Bacon fat   about 3 tablespoons
Onion   4 tablespoons minced
Celery   4 tablespoons minced
Green pepper   2 tablespoons minced
Mushrooms   ½ cup coarsely chopped
Rhubarb   1 cup finely diced
Flour   3 tablespoons
Canned tomatoes   ¾ cup drained
Beef bouillon   ½ cup
Salt   ½ teaspoon
Eggs   6, hard-cooked and sliced in rings
Cracker crumbs   1 cup
Parmesan cheese   ¼ cup grated
Margarine   ⅓ cup, melted
Toast or rice

Preheat oven to 350°. Fry bacon; use remaining bacon fat to sauté onion, celery, green pepper, mushrooms, and rhubarb. When soft, blend in flour; add tomatoes, bouillon, and salt, simmering for a few minutes until thick. Make alternate layers of sliced eggs and sauce in greased individual casseroles. Top with crumbled bacon. Mix together cracker crumbs, cheese, and margarine, and sprinkle over top. Bake for 15 minutes until sizzling hot. Can be served on toast. Serves 4.

Brunch Eggs Guadalajara

Bacon slices 2, diced
Bacon fat
Garlic clove ½, minced
Onion 3 tablespoons chopped
Green pepper 2 tablespoons chopped
Tomatoes 1 cup canned, drained
Rhubarb sauce (see Index) ½ cup unsweetened
Salt ½ teaspoon
Chili powder 1 teaspoon
Oregano ¼ cup
Worcestershire sauce 1 teaspoon
Green chili pepper 1 tablespoon chopped
Eggs 3 or 6
Cheddar cheese 3 tablespoons grated

Preheat oven to 350°. Fry bacon until almost crisp; remove. In bacon fat sauté garlic, onion, and green pepper until soft. Add tomatoes, rhubarb, seasonings, Worcestershire sauce and chili pepper. Grease 3 individual serving dishes; pour sauce in them and place in oven until bubbling. Then break 1 or 2 eggs in each dish, sprinkle cheese over, and bake for 12 minutes. Watch that yolk does not become too hard. Serves 3 heartily.

Whipped Cream-Cheese Omelet

Bacon slices   3, diced
Eggs   4
Unflavored yogurt   3 tablespoons
Salt   ½ teaspoon
Worcestershire sauce   ¼ teaspoon
Cream cheese   1 3-ounce package at room temperature
Rhubarb sauce (see Index)   ¼ cup sweetened and drained
Nutmeg   ⅛ teaspoon
Bacon fat

Fry bacon in flip-type omelet pan, or in skillet with rounded edges, until light brown. Beat eggs with yogurt, salt, and Worcestershire sauce until very fluffy. Cream together cheese, rhubarb, and nutmeg. Bacon grease should be sizzling in omelet pan. (Add margarine if needed.) Pour egg mixture in and cook as usual, lifting edges so that uncooked egg can flow underneath; do not overcook. When done, spread cream cheese mixture on ½ of omelet; flip pan shut, and remove. Or turn out omelet from skillet, spread on cream cheese mixture, and fold other side over. Cut in 2 parts. Serves 2.

Fantastic Fromage

Rhubarb sauce (see Index)   1 ½ cups slightly sweetened and drained
Cheddar cheese   ¼ cup shredded
Wheat germ   2 to 3 tablespoons
Walnuts   ¼ cup chopped

Preheat oven to 325°. Put ⅓ of the rhubarb and ½ the cheese into a buttered 1-quart casserole. Sprinkle with ½ the wheat germ. Repeat, finishing with rhubarb; top with nuts. Bake until piping hot for about 10 minutes. Serve hot with a vegetable salad for a meatless meal. Serves 3 to 4.

Bazaar Noodles

Noodles   4 ounces, cooked until tender in salted water
Cottage cheese   ½ cup
Egg   1, separated
Margarine   2 tablespoons, melted
Brown sugar   3 tablespoons
Sour cream or unflavored yogurt   ½ cup
Raisins   ¼ cup chopped
Walnuts   ½ cup chopped
Salt   to taste
Rhubarb sauce (see Index)   ½ cup sweetened and drained

Preheat oven to 350°. Combine noodles with cottage cheese. Mix together egg yolk and other ingredients except for egg white; stir into noodles, mixing well. Beat the egg white until stiff and fold gently into noodle mixture. Pour into 1½-quart buttered casserole. Bake for about 25 minutes. Serves 4.

Fruited Lentil Beanpot

Lentils   1 16-ounce package
Water   6 cups
Onion   1 cup chopped
Carrots   2, scraped and sliced into thick rounds
Salt   1 teaspoon
Ham bone or chunk of salt pork
Rhubarb   2 cups diced
Brown sugar   ¼ cup
Catsup   ¼ cup
Molasses   ¼ cup
Dry mustard   1 teaspoon

Wash lentils. In large kettle combine lentils, water, onion, carrots, salt, and ham bone; bring to a boil. Cover and simmer for 1 hour. Stir in remaining ingredients. Place in bean pot or Dutch oven. Bake at 350° for 1 hour or longer; stir occasionally. Serves 8 to 10.

Pilaf Plus

Uncooked spaghetti   ¼ cup broken into 1- to 2-inch pieces
Onion   2 tablespoons chopped
Margarine   4 tablespoons, melted
Bulgur wheat   1 cup
Chicken broth   2 cups
Salt   ½ teaspoon
Basil   ½ teaspoon
Marjoram   ¼ teaspoon
Rhubarb   ¾ cup finely diced
Raisins   ¼ cup
Slivered almonds   ¼ cup blanched

Brown spaghetti and onion in margarine. Add bulgur and stir until it is coated and golden. Add other ingredients except for almonds; bring to a boil and then cover and turn heat low; let cook for 20 minutes. It can stand covered for another 10 or 15 minutes. To serve, sprinkle with almonds. Serves 6.

Triple Bean Bake

Bacon slices   6*
Bacon fat
Green pepper   ½ cup chopped
Onion   1 cup chopped
Garlic clove   1, minced
Molasses   ¼ cup
Dry mustard   1 teaspoon
Salt   ½ teaspoon
Worcestershire sauce   1 tablespoon
Catsup or barbecue sauce   ½ cup
Rhubarb   1½ cups diced
Pork and beans   1 2-pound can
Kidney beans   1 16-ounce can, drained and liquid saved
Garbanzo beans   1 16-ounce can, drained and liquid saved

Preheat oven to 300°. Fry bacon until crisp; crumble. Sauté green pepper, onion, and garlic in bacon fat. Mix together molasses, dry mustard, salt, Worcestershire sauce, and catsup. Put the rhubarb and 3 kinds of beans in greased 3-quart casserole, mixing well. Stir in the onion mixture, bacon, and seasoning mixture. Bake for 30 minutes or more, until piping hot; add bean liquid if it becomes dry. Serves 6 to 8.

*Meats such as sausage, ham, wieners, can be added if desired.

Variation: Serve the beans in parboiled green peppers (1 for each person). Top them, remove seeds and pith, and parboil for 5 minutes in boiling salted water. Fill with beans and bake at 350° for 15 minutes.

Budget Garbanzo Cutlets

Garbanzo beans   1 16-ounce can
Rhubarb sauce (see Index)   ⅓ cup unsweetened
Salt   1 teaspoon
Parsley sprigs   3, chopped
Worcestershire sauce   1 teaspoon
Prepared mustard   ½ teaspoon
Lemon juice   1 tablespoon
Egg   1, hard-cooked and chopped
Egg   1, beaten
Walnuts   ½ cup chopped
Oregano   ¼ teaspoon
Garlic clove   1, minced
Whole wheat flour   2 or more tablespoons
Fine dry bread crumbs   ½ cup
Bacon fat or other meat drippings   4 tablespoons
Catsup or barbecue sauce   garnish

Pass garbanzos through a food mill. Mix in other ingredients except for flour, crumbs, bacon fat, and catsup. Add enough flour to make a fairly stiff dough. Form patties and dip in bread crumbs. Fry in bacon fat until crusty and brown on each side. To serve, cover with catsup. Makes 4 to 6.

Red, White, and Green Rice

Onion ½ cup chopped
Margarine 4 tablespoons, melted
Garlic clove 1, minced
Rhubarb ¾ cup finely diced
Rice 2 cups cooked
Rosemary ¼ teaspoon crumbled
Thyme ½ teaspoon crumbled
Basil ½ teaspoon crumbled
Cheddar cheese 1½ cups shredded
Unflavored yogurt ½ cup
Fresh or frozen peas 1 cup cooked just tender
Slivered almonds 1 cup toasted and blanched
Bread crumbs ½ cup

Preheat oven to 325°. Sauté onion in margarine until soft. Add garlic, rhubarb, and rice, and sauté for a few minutes. Add spices, ¾ cup of cheese, and yogurt, and heat through. Then carefully stir in peas. Add ¾ cup almonds. Turn into a greased 2-quart casserole; top with remaining cheese and nuts. Sprinkle with bread crumbs. Bake for 5 to 10 minutes to melt cheese and heat. Serves 4.

Desserts

Whole Wheat Chocolate Chippies

Margarine ½ cup
Brown sugar ¾ cup
Eggs 2
Vanilla 1 teaspoon
Whole wheat flour 1¼ cups unsifted
Ginger 1 teaspoon
Salt ¾ teaspoon
Baking soda 1 teaspoon
Lemon peel 1 tablespoon grated
Chocolate chips 1 cup
Walnuts 1 cup chopped
Rhubarb 1 cup finely chopped

Preheat oven to 350°. Cream together margarine, sugar, eggs, and vanilla until well blended. Add flour mixed with ginger, salt, soda, and lemon peel; mix well. Mix in chocolate chips, nuts, and rhubarb. Drop from teaspoon onto Teflon-coated or greased cookie sheet 2 inches apart. Bake 10 to 12 minutes until lightly browned. Remove from cookie sheet and place on wire rack to cool. Makes about 4 dozen.

Drops Waikiki

Margarine ¾ cup
Sugar 1 cup
Brown sugar 1 cup
Eggs 2, slightly beaten
Crushed pineapple ½ cup drained
Rhubarb sauce (see Index) ½ cup sweetened and drained
Flour 4 cups sifted
Salt ½ teaspoon
Baking soda 1 teaspoon
Ginger 1 teaspoon
Vanilla 2 teaspoons
Walnuts or pecans 1 cup chopped

Preheat oven to 350°. Cream together margarine and sugars; add eggs and blend well. Stir in fruit. Sift together dry ingredients; add to other mixture. Add vanilla and nuts. Drop on greased or Teflon cookie sheets. Bake for 12 minutes until lightly browned. Makes about 6 dozen.

Rich Rhubarb Squares

Margarine ½ cup
Brown sugar 1 cup
Flour 1½ cups
Salt ½ teaspoon
Cinnamon 1 teaspoon
Baking soda 1 teaspoon
Quick cooking oats 1½ cups
Water 1 tablespoon
Rhubarb sauce (see Index) 2 cups sweetened with honey and
    drained
Walnuts 1 cup chopped

Preheat oven to 350°. Cut margarine into sugar with pastry blender. Sift flour, salt, cinnamon, and soda and blend into margarine mixture with pastry blender. Add oats and water; mix until crumbly. Butter a 9 by 13-inch baking pan. Put ½ the crumb mixture into pan. Spread evenly with rhubarb sauce. Sprinkle nuts over mixture. Sprinkle remaining crumbs and press down. Bake 25 to 30 minutes. When cool, cut into bars or squares.

Chewy Overnight Chocobarbs

Egg whites 2
Sugar ⅔ cup
Salt dash
Carob powder or cocoa ¼ cup
Rhubarb sauce (see Index) ⅔ cup sweetened and drained through
    sieve
Walnuts ½ cup chopped
Vanilla 1 teaspoon

Preheat oven to 400°. With rotary beater, beat egg whites until foamy. Gradually beat in mixture of sugar, salt, and carob powder until mixture is very thick (as it would be for a meringue). Then add the well-drained rhubarb, nuts, and vanilla. Make 2 dozen small mounds on greased, foil-covered baking sheet. Put baking sheet in oven and turn heat off at once. Leave overnight. Do not open oven at all until morning.

Zucchinied Sour Cream Squares

Brown sugar   ¾ cup, firmly packed
Margarine   ¼ cup
Egg   1
Vanilla   1 teaspoon
Whole wheat flour   1 cup
Baking soda   ½ teaspoon
Salt   ¼ teaspoon
Dairy sour cream   ½ cup*
Lemon peel   ½ teaspoon
Rhubarb   ½ cup finely diced
Zucchini   ½ cup finely diced
Sugar   ¼ cup
Walnuts   ½ cup chopped
Margarine   1 tablespoon
Cinnamon   ½ teaspoon

Preheat oven to 350°. Cream together brown sugar and margarine. Blend in egg and vanilla. Stir together flour, soda, and salt; add to creamed mixture alternately with sour cream. Add lemon peel, rhubarb, and zucchini, and mix well. Turn into greased and floured 8-inch square baking pan. Mix rest of the ingredients together until crumbly; sprinkle over batter. Bake for 45 minutes; cool in pan. Cut in squares.
*Do not use homemade sour cream.

Rick's Rapid Rhubars

Graham crackers   1 4-ounce package
Walnuts   1 cup chopped
Margarine   ½ cup
Egg yolk   1
Brown sugar   ½ cup
Sugar   ½ cup
Vanilla   1 teaspoon
Ginger   ½ teaspoon
Rhubarb sauce (see Index)   ½ cup unsweetened and drained

Crush crackers and add walnuts. In a small saucepan, bring the
remaining ingredients to a simmer, stirring constantly, and let cook
for about 2 minutes until partially thickened. Butter an 8-inch square
pan. Pour in crumb and nut mixture; add hot fruit mixture. Blend
well; press down well. Chill. Cut into squares. This is a rich dessert
that should be kept in the refrigerator.

Lemony Rhubarb Glories

Flour   1 cup
Sugar   ¼ cup
Margarine   ½ cup
Sugar   1 cup
Flour   3 tablespoons
Eggs   2, well beaten
Lemon peel   1 teaspoon grated
Lemon juice   3 tablespoons
Rhubarb sauce (see Index)   ½ cup sweetened and drained or
　　Rhubarb   1 cup finely diced
Shredded coconut   ½ cup
Vanilla   1 teaspoon
Powdered sugar   sprinkle
Whipping cream   whipped

Preheat oven to 350°. For crust, mix 1 cup flour and ¼ cup sugar.
Cut in margarine with pastry blender; mix well with fingers. Press

into greased 8-inch square pan. Bake 15 minutes. Meanwhile, mix 1 cup sugar and 3 tablespoons flour. Beat them into eggs; mix in next 6 ingredients. Pour this mixture over hot baked crust and return to oven for about 30 minutes. Cool in pan. Sprinkle with powdered sugar. Cut in small squares for cookies or in larger pieces for dessert. Top with whipped cream if desired.

Old-Fashioned Ginger Cookies

Margarine   ½ cup
Sugar   1 cup
Egg   1, well beaten
Molasses   ¼ cup
Vinegar   1½ teaspoons
Flour   2 cups
Baking soda   1 teaspoon
Ginger   2 teaspoons
Cloves   ⅛ teaspoon
Cinnamon   ½ teaspoon
Rhubarb sauce (see Index)   ⅓ cup slightly sweetened and drained
Walnuts   1 cup halves or larger chunks

Preheat oven to 325°. Cream margarine and sugar. Beat in egg, molasses, and vinegar. Sift dry ingredients together and add to egg mixture; add rhubarb sauce. Drop by small spoonfuls on greased or Teflon-coated cookie sheet 2 inches apart. Press a nut in each mound. Bake about 15 minutes. For a softer cookie, bake for a little less time. Makes 4 dozen.

Del's Date Dainties

Eggs 2
Brown sugar ¾ cup
Flour ⅔ cup sifted
Baking powder 1 teaspoon
Cinnamon ½ teaspoon
Baking soda 1 teaspoon
Salt ¼ teaspoon
Dates ⅓ cup pitted and cut in small pieces
Rhubarb sauce (see Index) ⅔ cup unsweetened and drained
Lemon juice 1 tablespoon
Vanilla 1 teaspoon
Walnuts 1 cup coarsely chopped
Powdered sugar enough to dust cookies

Preheat oven to 350°. Beat eggs with rotary beater until they are thick and lemon colored; slowly beat in sugar. Sift together dry ingredients; add them to egg mixture, stirring in with spoon. Blend in the rest of the ingredients. Pour into a greased 8-inch square pan that has waxed paper on the bottom. Bake for 25 minutes. Invert onto cooling rack at once and remove waxed paper. Cut in squares. Roll in powdered sugar.

Crunchy Drops

Margarine 1 cup
Brown sugar 1 ¼ cups
Eggs 2
Vanilla 1 teaspoon
Rhubarb sauce (see Index) 1 cup sweetened and drained
Flour 2 cups sifted
Baking soda ½ teaspoon
Salt ½ teaspoon
Mace ⅛ teaspoon
Quick cooking oats 2 cups
Walnuts 1 cup chopped

Preheat oven to 350°. Cream margarine with sugar. Beat in eggs, vanilla, and rhubarb sauce until smooth. Add dry ingredients sifted together; blend in oats and nuts. Drop by teaspoons onto greased or Teflon-coated cookie sheet. Bake until golden brown (12 or 13 minutes). Remove from cookie sheet and cool on wire racks. Makes about 4 dozen.

Fabulous Fridge Fudge

Cream cheese 1 3-ounce package at room temperature
Powdered sugar 2½ cups sifted
Rhubarb sauce (see Index) 4 tablespoons sweetened and drained
Almonds ½ cup chopped, blanched, and toasted

Whip the cream cheese until fluffy. Gradually beat in powdered sugar, adding 1 tablespoon of rhubarb sauce twice when needed for moistening. Add the almonds last. Spread fudge in a buttered 8-inch square pan. Spread remaining rhubarb sauce in a thin layer over top. Chill overnight; fudge stiffens very well after the chilling. Keep it in refrigerator.

Fandango Nut Balls

Walnuts ½ cup coarsely chopped
Raisins 1 cup, chopped or fairly finely ground
Rhubarb sauce (see Index) 1 cup sweetened and drained
Dry powdered milk 1 cup
Chocolate chips ⅔ cup
Oatmeal 1 cup, powdered in blender after measuring
Walnuts 1 cup finely chopped

Mix coarsely chopped ½ cup of nuts with the other ingredients, reserving about ⅓ of the oatmeal, and the finely chopped nuts. Mix the candy well with hands. Add reserved oatmeal and more dry milk if necessary so that candy is not sticky. (Amount of thickening required depends upon consistency of rhubarb sauce.) Form into walnut-sized balls and dip each in remaining nuts. Or butter an 8 by 8-inch pan; sprinkle ½ the finely chopped nuts on the bottom of the pan; spread the candy in pan; cover with rest of nuts. Press them in with hand; chill. Then cut into squares.

Cocobarbary Bars

Margarine   1 tablespoon melted
Dark corn syrup   3 tablespoons
Rhubarb sauce (see Index)   ½ cup unsweetened and drained
Flaked coconut   ½ cup
Vanilla   ½ teaspoon
Powdered milk   1 cup
Graham cracker or vanilla wafer crumbs   1 cup
Walnuts   ½ cup chopped
Powdered sugar   sifted, for dusting candy

Combine margarine, corn syrup, rhubarb, coconut, and vanilla; mix well. Stir in powdered milk and then add crumbs and nuts to make a very stiff dough. Add more milk or crumbs if necessary. Chill for 2 hours. Form into 3 logs or into balls, sprinkling outside with powdered sugar. Keep chilled. Slice logs to desired portions.

Pieces of 'Ade

Sugar   2 cups
Rhubarb   2 cups diced, then finely ground
Orange   1, coarsely grated peel, juice, and pulp
Lemon   1, coarsely grated peel, juice, and pulp
Unflavored gelatin   1 tablespoon
Water   ¼ cup
Walnuts   1¼ cups finely chopped

Sprinkle sugar over rhubarb and let stand for 1 hour, stirring occasionally. Heat rhubarb over medium heat until it comes to a boil; add orange and lemon. Simmer for 45 minutes, stirring occasionally, until thick as jam. Dissolve gelatin in water; add a little of jam mixture, stirring well. Add this to hot mixture, cooking until well dissolved (about 5 minutes). Transfer to a shallow bowl and chill until quite firm. Form 3 logs and roll them in nuts; chill overnight. Slice as needed and keep chilled.

Yorkshireman's Delight

Whole wheat flour   ¼ cup
Flour   ½ cup
Salt   ¼ teaspoon
Baking powder   ¼ teaspoon
Cinnamon   ¼ teaspoon
Evaporated milk   1 cup
Egg   1, beaten
Vanilla   ¼ teaspoon
Honey   1 tablespoon
Margarine   2 tablespoons
Rhubarb   1 cup finely diced
Brown sugar sauce (see Index)   omit rhubarb in it
Vanilla ice cream or rich cream

Put whole wheat flour in a deep mixing bowl; add dry ingredients sifted together. Mix milk, egg, vanilla, and honey with rotary beater. Stir into dry ingredients, mixing with beater. (Batter can now be chilled for an hour, if desired, and beaten again before baking.) Melt margarine in a 9-inch pie pan in a 375° oven until margarine sizzles. Then pour batter in quickly and add rhubarb. Push it down and cover with batter. Bake at 375° for about 30 minutes. Serve warm with Brown Sugar Sauce and vanilla ice cream. Serves 6.

Spring-in-a-Dish Compote

Rhubarb sauce (see Index)   2 cups sweetened
Strawberries   ½ cup, unsweetened and sliced if large
Blueberries   ¼ cup
Small cantaloupe balls   ½ cup
Burgundy or rosé wine   ¼ cup
Whipping cream   whipped

Mix fruits, add wine, and gently shake to mix without mushing fruit. Chill for 1 hour or more. Serve with a mound of whipped cream. Serves 4 to 6.

Winey Brown Barby

Rhubarb   1½ cups finely chopped
Burgundy or dry red wine   ⅔ cup
Graham cracker or bread crumbs   1½ cups
Margarine   ¼ cup, melted
Brown sugar   ¾ cup
Orange peel   2 tablespoons grated
Walnuts   ⅔ cup chopped
Cinnamon   ½ teaspoon
Ginger   ¼ teaspoon
Nutmeg   ¼ teaspoon
Salt   ½ teaspoon

Preheat oven to 350°. Spread ½ the rhubarb in a buttered 1-quart casserole. Sprinkle ½ the wine over rhubarb. Combine other ingredients, mixing well. Sprinkle ½ the crumb mixture over rhubarb-wine mixture. Add rest of rhubarb; pour remaining wine over it; sprinkle the other ½ of the crumb mixture over. Bake covered for 15 minutes. Then remove cover and bake for 10 minutes more. Serves 4 to 5.

Note: This is delicious served hot with ice cream over it.

Danish Fluff

Rhubarb sauce (see Index) 1½ cups sweetened
Cornstarch 1½ tablespoons
Dry wine or orange juice 1½ tablespoons
Salt dash
Egg 1, separated
Ginger root 1 teaspoon grated
Walnuts ¼ cup chopped
Sugar 2 tablespoons
Graham cracker crumbs ¼ cup
Margarine 2 tablespoons, melted

Combine rhubarb sauce with cornstarch that has been dissolved in wine; add salt. Cook for several minutes, stirring constantly, until thick and clear. Cool slightly; stir in beaten egg yolk, ginger root, and walnuts. While it cools, beat the egg white with sugar to stiff peak stage; fold into rhubarb mixture. Spoon into 4 individual serving dishes and chill. Mix crumbs and margarine, and sprinkle over pudding before serving. Serves 4.

Rhubarb Delicioso

Graham cracker crumbs ⅔ cup
Walnuts ½ cup chopped
Powdered sugar 3 tablespoons
Cinnamon ¼ teaspoon
Margarine 4 tablespoons
Honey ⅔ cup
Egg 1, slightly beaten
Vanilla ½ teaspoon
Lemon peel 1 teaspoon grated
Flour 3 tablespoons
Salt ¼ teaspoon
Rhubarb 1 cup finely diced
Ice cream or whipping cream

Preheat oven to 350°. Mix first 5 ingredients together and press into a 9-inch pie pan. Bake until light brown (about 6 minutes). Mix honey, egg, vanilla, and lemon peel together until smooth. Stir flour and salt into rhubarb and add to honey mixture. Pour rhubarb mixture onto crust and bake another 25 minutes until just set. Serve with ice cream if desired. Serves 6.

Robbie's Rhubarb Refresher

Rhubarb sauce (see Index) 1 cup sweetened and drained
Ginger ¼ teaspoon
Fresh strawberries 1 cup quartered and unsweetened
Orange peel ½ teaspoon grated
Unflavored yogurt 1 cup
Fresh mint sprigs 4

Gently fold first 4 ingredients into yogurt; be careful not to mash fruit. Chill well in a metal bowl. Garnish with mint. Serves 4.

Rice Pudding Extraordinaire

Water ¼ cup
Rice ¼ cup, washed
Margarine 1 tablespoon
Salt ¼ teaspoon
Milk 1½ cups
Unflavored gelatin 2 teaspoons
Rum or sherry 3 tablespoons
Vanilla ½ teaspoon
Rhubarb sauce (see Index) 1 cup sweetened and drained
Brown sugar ⅓ cup
Slivered almonds 4 tablespoons blanched

Bring water to a boil in small saucepan. Add rice, margarine, and salt; simmer over moderate heat until water is absorbed, stirring often. Add milk. Transfer to a double boiler and cook covered over boiling water for about 1½ hours, stirring occasionally, until milk is well absorbed and rice is tender. Soften gelatin in rum and stir into hot rice. Add vanilla, rhubarb sauce, and brown sugar and stir well. Chill. Sprinkle with almonds and serve. Serves 4.

Chocolate Rhubarb Imperiale

Margarine   ½ cup
Sugar   ½ cup
Cocoa or carob powder   2 tablespoons
Cinnamon   ¼ teaspoon
Rhubarb sauce (see Index)   ½ cup sweetened, moderately liquid
Egg   1
Unflavored yogurt   ¼ cup
Vanilla   ½ teaspoon
Walnuts   ½ cup coarsely chopped
Graham cracker crumbs   ⅓ cup
Raspberry or strawberry jam   ⅓ cup

Melt margarine in a heavy saucepan. Mix sugar, cocoa, and cinnamon; stir into rhubarb sauce. Then stir egg, yogurt, and vanilla into rhubarb mixture, beating well. Blend this mixture into melted margarine and heat just to the boiling point; do not overcook. Remove from heat; stir in nuts and crumbs. Spoon into individual serving dishes. Chill. Before serving, spread a thin glaze of raspberry or strawberry jam over the top. Serves 4.

Note: This is best when served the same day it is made.

Banana Jubilee

Margarine   2 tablespoons
Brown sugar   ¼ cup
Sherry, rum, or bourbon   2 tablespoons
Rhubarb sauce (see Index)   ⅓ cup unsweetened
Ripe bananas   4, halved lengthwise
Ice cream   for topping
Pecans   3 tablespoons, chopped

Melt margarine in a heavy skillet. Add sugar and stir until melted. Add sherry and rhubarb sauce. Add bananas and simmer at medium heat, turning carefully several times, for about 10 minutes. Serve warm in the syrup, topped with ice cream and nuts. Delicious warm or cold. Serves 4.

Sauced Strawberry Amandine

Sponge, angel, or pound cake   4 pieces 3-inches square
Sherry or rum   ¼ cup
Jell-O Vanilla Instant Pudding & Pie Filling mix   1 4½-ounce
   package
Milk   2 cups, chilled
Rhubarb sauce (see Index)   ¾ cup sweetened and chilled
Strawberries   ½ cup sliced
Whipped cream   1 cup, whipped
Slivered almonds   ¼ cup toasted and blanched

In 4 individual serving dishes, arrange the cake cubes. Drizzle a tablespoon of sherry over each piece of cake; let stand while you beat up pudding mix in milk. Spread rhubarb sauce over cake. Top with a layer of pudding. Add strawberries and then whipped cream. Sprinkle almonds over top. This dish can sit for hours before serving. Serves 4.

Regina's Doce Brasileiro*

Rhubarb sauce (see Index)   ¾ cup sweetened, drained, and chilled
Vanilla ice cream   1 pint, slightly softened
Shredded coconut   1 cup
Almonds   ¾ cup blanched and chopped

Preheat oven to 250°. Quickly stir the rhubarb sauce into ice cream; transfer to an ice cube tray, and return to freezer to firm up. Spread coconut and almonds on a cookie sheet and place in oven for a few minutes to toast. Watch carefully so they do not burn; they should be golden; spread them on a plate to cool. Cut ice cream into 4 squares; lift them out onto the coconut and nuts. Cover each ice cream mold thickly with mixture. Serve at once or return to freezer. Makes 4.
*This is a delectable Brazilian dessert.

Sherried Rhuberry

Strawberry-banana Jell-O   1 3-ounce package
Water   ¾ cup
Rhubarb sauce (see Index)   ½ cup sweetened
Lemon juice   2 teaspoons
Sherry   ½ cup
Vanilla ice cream   4 spoonfuls

Dissolve Jell-O in boiling water. Add rhubarb, lemon juice, and sherry. Pour into individual molds; chill until firm. Turn out of molds and top with a spoonful of ice cream. Serves 4.

Butter Pecan Sherried Ice Cream

Pecans   1 cup chopped
Whole pecans   4
Margarine   1 tablespoon
Rhubarb sauce (see Index)   1 cup cooked with fresh mint leaves, slightly sweetened, and drained
Sherry or Marsala wine   3 tablespoons
Vanilla ice cream   1 pint, softened

Sauté both chopped and whole pecans in margarine for a few minutes; let cool. Remove mint leaves from rhubarb. Stir rhubarb, wine, and cooled chopped nuts into the vanilla ice cream. Freeze in small serving dishes until firm. Top each with a whole pecan. Serves 4.

Soft Frozen Velvet

Honey ⅓ cup
Unflavored gelatin 1 teaspoon
Orange juice ⅓ cup
Rhubarb purée (see Index) ½ cup sweetened
Unflavored yogurt 2 cups
Orange peel ½ teaspoon grated

Mix honey, gelatin, orange juice, and rhubarb in a small pan. Let stand for a few minutes to soften gelatin; heat and stir to dissolve gelatin. Transfer to a large bowl and cool. Then stir in yogurt and orange peel; chill. Pour into an ice cube tray when it is well chilled. Freeze for about 1 hour. Stir every 15 minutes or whenever mixture starts to stiffen around edges. When it is the consistency of soft ice cream, transfer from ice cube compartment to main section of freezer until served. Serves 4.

Frosted Avocado Brasilia

Large avocado 1, peeled and seeded
Salt ½ teaspoon
Lemon juice 2 tablespoons
Lemon peel ½ teaspoon grated
Honey ¼ cup
Rhubarb sauce (see Index) ¾ cup sweetened
Unflavored yogurt ¾ cup

Mix all together in blender and whirl until smooth. Freeze in 1 ice cube tray. Stir from time to time. Serve slightly soft. Serves 4.

Frosty Wine Sherbet

Unflavored gelatin   1 teaspoon
Rosé or pink chablis wine   2 cups*
Rhubarb purée (see Index)   1 cup sweetened
Lemon juice   1 tablespoon

Soften gelatin in ¼ cup wine. Heat the rest of wine to a simmer; dissolve softened gelatin in it and cool. Add rhubarb and lemon juice and pour into 1 ice cube tray. Freeze, stirring every 15 minutes or so, for about 2 hours. Let it soften to a slush before serving. Serves 4 to 6.
*Different wines can be used to vary the flavor.

Rhubarb Ice Ana Maria

Frozen orange juice concentrate   1 6-ounce can
Water   2 cups
Light corn syrup   1 cup
Rhubarb purée (see Index)   1½ cups sweetened

Mix all ingredients together and freeze for several hours in 2 ice cube trays. Just before serving, remove from trays, chop up, and let soften but not melt. Serve at once. Serves 6 to 8.

Ummmmmm Popsicles

Unflavored yogurt   1 8-ounce cup
Apple sauce   ½ cup
Rhubarb sauce (see Index)   1 cup sweetened

Mix all together well and freeze in popsicle molds or in ice cube tray; insert toothpicks once popsicles start to freeze. They can be eaten in a dish by breaking up the frozen sauce to soften it before eating.

Rhubarb Crème

Rhubarb 2 cups finely diced
Sugar ½ cup
Evaporated milk or half 'n' half 1 cup
Eggs 2, separated
Lemon peel 1 teaspoon grated
Lemon juice 1 tablespoon
Vanilla 1 teaspoon
Sugar ⅓ cup

Sprinkle rhubarb with sugar and let stand for 1 hour. Simmer without water for 5 minutes until tender; cool. Mix together milk, beaten yolks, lemon peel and juice, and vanilla. Blend in cooled rhubarb. Freeze in 1 ice cube tray until firm. Beat the whites until frothy; gradually add the ⅓ cup sugar and beat until peaks are stiff. Turn out the frozen rhubarb mixture and break it up; beat with rotary beater until smooth but not melted. Fold in stiff whites. Return to tray and freeze again until firm. Before serving, let it stand at room temperature for 10 minutes. Serves 6.

Marilyn's Mincemeat Deluxe

Tart apples   6 cups peeled, cored, and diced
Rhubarb   6 cups sliced in 1-inch pieces
Raisins   4 cups
Mixed candied fruit   1½ cups diced
Pitted dates   1 cup chopped
Sugar   7 cups
Orange juice   1½ cups
Orange peel   grated from 2 oranges
Lemon juice   4 tablespoons
Molasses   ¾ cup
Fresh ginger root   1 tablespoon grated
Cinnamon   2 teaspoons
Allspice   2 teaspoons
Cloves   2 teaspoons
Nutmeg   1 teaspoon

Mix all together and bring to a boil, stirring until well blended. Simmer gently 35 to 40 minutes until it thickens. Fill 4 sterilized quart jars, seal, and process in boiling water bath for 15 minutes. Enough for 4 pies.

Note: Any leftover sauce can be used on ice cream.

Sour Cream Cheese Pie

Sugar ⅔ cup
Cornstarch 2 tablespoons
Ginger ½ teaspoon
Rhubarb 3 cups finely diced
Pastry 1 9-inch crust
Cream cheese 1 8-ounce package
Egg 1, slightly beaten
Sugar ½ cup
Nutmeg ⅛ teaspoon
Dairy sour cream 1 cup*
Orange peel 1 teaspoon grated
Brown sugar 2 tablespoons
Slivered almonds ¼ cup blanched and toasted

Preheat oven to 425°. Mix the sugar, cornstarch, and ginger. Add to rhubarb and blend well. Turn into pie crust and bake 15 minutes. Meanwhile, whip the cream cheese with fork until fluffy. Add egg, sugar, and nutmeg. Blend well. Reduce oven heat to 350° while you spread cream cheese layer on baked rhubarb filling. Return pie to oven and bake 20 minutes longer; cool. Chill several hours or overnight. Then spread on the sour cream mixed with orange peel and sugar. Sprinkle with almonds. Keep refrigerated until served.
*Do not use homemade sour cream.

Spring Pie Supreme

Sugar 1½ cups
Flour 3 tablespoons
Nutmeg ½ teaspoon
Orange peel ½ teaspoon grated
Margarine 1 tablespoon, melted
Eggs 2, beaten
Rhubarb 3 cups finely diced
Walnuts ½ cup chopped (optional)
Pastry 1 9-inch crust
Egg whites 2
Salt ¼ teaspoon
Cream of tartar ¼ teaspoon
Sugar 3 tablespoons
Vanilla ½ teaspoon

Mix together 1½ cups sugar, flour, nutmeg, and orange peel. Add margarine and eggs. Add rhubarb and walnuts and mix well; fill pie crust. Bake for 10 minutes at 425°, and then 30 minutes at 325°. Prepare meringue topping by beating egg whites and salt until frothy. Then beat in cream of tartar until whites are stiff but not dry. Beat in sugar a teaspoon at a time; beat in vanilla. Do not overbeat. Spread over hot pie and return to 325° oven for about 10 minutes.

Pluperfect Berry Pie

White sugar   1 cup
Brown sugar   ½ cup
Tapioca   3 tablespoons
Salt   ¼ teaspoon
Ginger   ¼ teaspoon
Rhubarb   3 cups finely diced
Large strawberries   2 cups, halved or quartered
Lemon peel   ¼ teaspoon grated
Orange juice   ¼ cup
Pastry   1 9-inch crust plus extra dough for top strips
Margarine   1 tablespoon

Preheat oven to 400°. Mix dry ingredients together. Mix in fruit, lemon peel, and orange juice; let stand, stirring occasionally, for 15 minutes. Pour fruit mixture into pie crust; dot with margarine. Cut 6 inch-wide strips of pastry so they are long enough to cross the top. Twist slightly and lay on top, pressing into edge of bottom crust. Bake for 35 minutes. If crust begins to brown too much, lay a sheet of foil on top to reflect the heat. Let cool well to thicken.

"See Red" Cream Pie

Sugar ½ cup
Cornstarch 5 teaspoons
Flour ¼ cup
Salt ½ teaspoon
Ginger ¼ teaspoon
Orange peel ½ teaspoon grated
Milk 2 cups
Egg 1, separated
Vanilla ½ teaspoon
Margarine 1 tablespoon
Strawberries 2 ½ cups sliced
Pastry 1 baked 9-inch pie shell
Rhubarb sauce (see Index) 1 cup sweetened and drained
Whipping cream whipped

Mix dry ingredients together in a saucepan. Add orange peel; gradually blend in milk. Over medium high heat, bring to boiling point while stirring. Then lower the heat and simmer, stirring, until quite thick. Stir some of hot mixture into beaten egg yolk, and return that mixture to saucepan. Bring to a boil again, stirring. Then remove from heat and add vanilla and margarine; chill. Whip the egg white until stiff and fold into chilled filling. Blend in the strawberries carefully, and pour into baked pie shell. Spread rhubarb sauce over top. Top with whipped cream if desired.

Arabian Night Delight

Rhubarb 2 cups finely diced
Sugar 1 cup
Tapioca 1½ tablespoons
Eggs 3, well beaten
Lemon juice 2 tablespoons
Orange peel 1 teaspoon grated
Cinnamon ½ teaspoon
Pecans or walnuts 1 cup chopped
Pitted dates 1 cup, chopped
Pastry enough for 9-inch crust and lattice top

Mix together everything but nuts, dates, and crust. Let stand for 15 minutes. Mix nuts and dates into rhubarb mixture; pour into pie shell; cover with lattice top. Bake at 425° for 10 minutes; reduce heat to 350° for another 30 minutes.

Cloud Nine Raisin Chiffon

Lemon Jell-O 1 3-ounce package
Water 1 cup, boiling
Honey 3 tablespoons
Raisins ⅓ cup
Rosé wine or sherry ¼ cup
Rhubarb sauce (see Index) ⅔ cup sweetened and drained
Walnuts ½ cup chopped
Egg whites 3
Sugar ¼ cup
Pastry 1 baked 9-inch pie shell

Dissolve jello in water. Add honey and raisins and let stand 10 minutes. Add wine; chill until almost set. Stir in rhubarb and nuts; return to refrigerator to chill while you beat whites with rotary beater to soft peak stage. Gradually beat in sugar; whip to stiff peak stage. Fold whites gently into rhubarb mixture. Spoon into pastry shell. Chill until firm.

Savannah Sweet Potato Pie

Pastry 1 9-inch pie shell
Sweet potatoes 3 cups peeled, cooked, and sliced
Rhubarb sauce (see Index) 1½ cups sweetened and drained
Brown sugar 1 cup
Cornstarch 4 teaspoons
Milk 1 cup
Salt ½ teaspoon
Margarine ¼ cup
Nutmeg ¼ teaspoon
Ginger ¼ teaspoon
Pecans 1 cup halves
Vanilla ice cream 1 pint

In the unbaked crust arrange sweet potatoes; spread hot rhubarb sauce over them. In a saucepan mix sugar and cornstarch, stir in milk gradually, and add other ingredients except for pecans and ice cream. Simmer until thick and smooth. Pour over sweet potato-rhubarb mixture in crust; top with pecans. Bake at 400° for 10 minutes, then another 10 minutes at 350°. Serve warm with ice cream.

Piquant Citrus Pie

Rhubarb   3½ cups finely diced
Honey   ¾ cup
Salt   ¼ teaspoon
Orange juice   3 tablespoons
Cornstarch   2 tablespoons
Water or orange juice   3 tablespoons
Lemon juice   1 tablespoon
Lemon peel   1 teaspoon grated
Eggs   2, separated
Pastry or crumb shell   1 baked 9-inch pie shell
Whipping cream   whipped

Cook rhubarb, honey, salt, and orange juice over low heat until it comes to a boil. Add cornstarch dissolved in water; cook, stirring constantly until thickened. Add lemon juice and peel. Beat egg yolks slightly; stir some of hot rhubarb mixture into them, and then stir this back into rhubarb; cool. Beat 2 egg whites until stiff and fold into rhubarb mixture. Pour into baked crust. Top with whipped cream if desired.

Cathy's Canadian Cupcakes

Flour   1 cup sifted
Cocoa or carob powder   1 tablespoon
Baking soda   ½ teaspoon
Cinnamon   ¼ teaspoon
Allspice   ¼ teaspoon
Margarine   ⅓ cup
Brown sugar   ⅔ cup
Egg   1
Vanilla   1 teaspoon
Dairy sour cream   ⅓ cup*
Rhubarb sauce (see Index)   ⅔ cup sweetened and drained
Walnuts   ⅓ cup chopped
Chocolate bits   ¼ cup

Preheat oven to 325°. Mix together flour, cocoa, soda, and spices. Cream margarine. Beat in sugar until fluffy, and then add egg and vanilla. Beat in sour cream. Add dry ingredients and beat until smooth. Fold in rhubarb, nuts, and chocolate bits. Fill cupcake papers lining muffin tins. Bake for 25 to 30 minutes. Remove from pan and let cool on wire rack. Makes 12.

*Do not use homemade sour cream.

Note: These are so rich they need no frosting.

Chocolate Velvet

Unsweetened baking chocolate   4 1-ounce squares
Margarine   1 cup
Flour   2 cups sifted
Baking soda   1 teaspoon
Ginger   1 teaspoon
Cinnamon   1 teaspoon
Cloves   ½ teaspoon
Brown sugar   1½ cups
Eggs   2
Vanilla   1 teaspoon
Rhubarb sauce (see Index)   1 cup slightly sweetened and drained
Unflavored yogurt   ½ cup
Walnuts   1 cup coarsely chopped

Preheat oven to 350°. Melt chocolate in heavy pan over very low heat with ½ of the margarine; stir constantly. Cool. Sift flour, baking soda, and spices. Cut sugar into rest of margarine with pastry blender. Beat in eggs 1 at a time. Stir in chocolate, vanilla, and rhubarb. Add flour mixture alternately with yogurt, beating until smooth after each addition. Stir in nuts. Grease a 9 by 13-inch baking pan and line bottom with waxed paper. Spread batter in pan. Bake for about 35 minutes. Cool in pan. Let stand overnight; texture improves with age. Frost with your favorite chocolate cream frosting.

McIntire Oatmeal Cake

Quick cooking oats ½ cup
Rhubarb purée (see Index) ¾ cup sweetened and fairly liquid
Sugar ¼ cup
Brown sugar ¼ cup
Salad oil ¼ cup
Egg 1
Flour ¾ cup
Baking soda ½ teaspoon
Salt ½ teaspoon
Baking powder 2½ teaspoons
Ginger ¼ teaspoon
Nutmeg ¼ teaspoon
Walnuts ½ cup chopped
Vanilla ½ teaspoon

Preheat oven to 350°. Mix oats and hot rhubarb purée; set aside. Beat together the sugars, oil, and egg. Sift dry ingredients together. After oatmeal mixture has sat for about 10 minutes, stir it into sugar mixture; add dry ingredients. Stir in walnuts and vanilla. Pour into greased 8-inch square pan that has waxed paper on bottom. Bake for about 30 minutes.
Variation: Spread the batter over 3 cups diced rhubarb that has stood in 1 cup sugar for an hour, and bake 30 to 40 minutes. Invert to serve and you have a rhubarb upside-down cake.

Sour Cream Dream Cake

Brown sugar   1½ cups
Margarine   ¾ cup
Eggs   2
Vanilla   1 teaspoon
Flour   2½ cups sifted
Baking soda   1 teaspoon
Salt   ½ teaspoon
Cinnamon   1 teaspoon
Evaporated milk   1 cup
Vinegar   2 tablespoons
Instant coffee powder   2 tablespoons
Walnuts   1 cup chopped
Rhubarb   2 cups finely chopped
Whipping cream   2 cups whipped or
    Favorite butter cream frosting   2 cups

Preheat oven to 350°. Cream together sugar and margarine. Beat in eggs and vanilla. Sift together flour, soda, salt, and cinnamon. Sour the evaporated milk with vinegar, and then stir in coffee powder. Add dry ingredients alternately with milk to creamed mixture, beating smooth after each addition. Stir in walnuts and rhubarb. Pour into 2 8-inch layer cake pans, the sides of which have been buttered and the bottom covered with waxed paper. Bake for 35 to 40 minutes. Let cool in pan for 10 minutes on a rack; then invert. Put together with whipped cream and frost tops and sides.

Deep South Yam Cake

Flour ¾ cup
Baking powder 1 ½ teaspoons
Baking soda ½ teaspoon
Salt 1 teaspoon
Cinnamon 1 teaspoon
Margarine ½ cup, soft
Brown sugar ½ cup
Yams or sweet potatoes ½ cup cooked and mashed
Rhubarb sauce (see Index) ½ cup sweetened and drained
Frozen orange juice concentrate ¼ cup, thawed
Egg 1, beaten
Orange peel ½ teaspoon grated
Vanilla 1 teaspoon
Raisins ½ cup
Walnuts or pecans ½ cup chopped
Unsweetened chocolate 1 1-ounce square, melted

Preheat oven to 350°. Sift together first 5 ingredients. Cream together margarine and sugar. Mix in rest of ingredients. Blend in flour mixture; batter will be rather stiff. Spread evenly into a greased 8-inch square pan with waxed paper on the bottom. Bake for about 25 minutes. Cool in pan, and frost as desired.

Gingery Graham Cake

Margarine   ½ cup at room temperature
Brown sugar   1 cup
Vanilla   1 teaspoon
Eggs   2
Flour   ¼ cup
Salt   ½ teaspoon
Baking soda   ½ teaspoon
Baking powder   2 teaspoons
Ginger   ½ teaspoon
Graham cracker crumbs   2 cups
Rhubarb sauce (see Index)   ⅔ cup sweetened and drained
Walnuts   ½ cup coarsely chopped
Dessert topping or any rhubarb frosting (see Index)

Preheat oven to 350°. Cream margarine and sugar together. Add vanilla and then eggs, 1 at a time. Sift together flour, salt, soda, baking powder, and ginger; add crumbs. Alternately add the dry mixture and the rhubarb to the creamed mixture, beating well after each addition. Add walnuts. Bake in a greased 9 by 12 by 2-inch pan, with waxed paper on bottom, for about 30 to 35 minutes. Test for doneness in center with toothpick. Let cool on wire rack for 10 minutes. Then invert and remove paper. Serve with dessert topping or frost with any rhubarb frosting.

Spring Tonic Cake

Brown sugar ¾ cup
Margarine ¼ cup
Egg 1
Vanilla 1 teaspoon
Flour 1 cup sifted
Baking soda ½ teaspoon
Salt ¼ teaspoon
Baking powder ½ teaspoon
Cinnamon ½ teaspoon
Ginger ¼ teaspoon
Orange juice ½ cup
Rhubarb 1 cup finely diced
Orange peel 1 tablespoon grated
Walnuts ½ cup chopped
Brown sugar ½ cup

Preheat oven to 325°. Mix sugar and margarine together using pastry blender; add egg and vanilla, stirring until blended. Sift dry ingredients together. Mix them into the sugar mixture alternately with orange juice. Stir in rhubarb and orange peel. Pour batter into a greased 8-inch round layer cake pan with waxed paper on bottom. Sprinkle with nuts and sugar. Bake for 35 minutes. Cool in pan for 10 minutes; turn out on wire rack. Needs no frosting.

Never-Fail Spice Cake

Whole wheat flour   1 cup
Flour   1½ cups
Brown sugar   ½ cup firmly packed
Honey   ¼ cup
Baking powder   2 teaspoons
Baking soda   1 teaspoon
Salt   1½ teaspoons
Cinnamon   1½ teaspoons
Ginger   ½ teaspoon
Cloves   ¼ teaspoon
Orange juice   ⅓ cup
Sherry   3 tablespoons
Salad oil   ¾ cup
Vanilla   2 teaspoons
Eggs   2
Rhubarb   2½ cups finely diced
Walnuts   1 cup chopped
Ice cream

Preheat oven to 325°. Mix everything except ice cream together in a large bowl in order given. Beat until smooth. Pour batter into greased 9 by 13-inch pan that has waxed paper on the bottom. Bake 45 minutes; cool in pan. Serve cold or warm with ice cream.

Crunchy Fill-or-Frost

Margarine ¼ cup
Honey ⅓ cup
Evaporated milk 3 tablespoons
Almonds or pecans ¼ cup chopped
Shredded coconut ¼ cup
Rhubarb sauce (see Index) ½ cup very sweet and drained
Vanilla ½ teaspoon
Salt pinch
Lemon peel ½ teaspoon grated

In a small pan melt margarine. Stir in honey and milk. Boil for 6 minutes, stirring constantly. Add other ingredients and simmer for a minute until hot; let cool a bit. Then spread between 2 layers or on top of 8-inch square cake.

Sweet-Sour Filling

Rhubarb sauce (see Index) 1 cup sweetened
Cornstarch 2 tablespoons
Honey 3 tablespoons
Salt ¼ teaspoon
Orange peel 1 teaspoon grated
Orange juice ½ cup
Lemon juice 2 teaspoons
Egg yolk 1, beaten
Margarine 1 tablespoon

Into the rhubarb sauce mix cornstarch, honey, salt, orange peel and juice, and lemon juice. Simmer over very low heat, stirring constantly, until clear and thick. Add a small amount of the hot mixture to egg yolk, and then return this to the pan. Simmer for another 2 minutes. Remove from heat and stir in margarine; cool. Spread between 2 layers of cake.

Quick Rhubarb Royale

Margarine   ¼ cup
Brown sugar   ½ cup
Rhubarb sauce (see Index)   ¼ cup sweetened and drained
Pecans or walnuts   1 cup
Shredded coconut   ½ cup

Blend margarine and sugar together. Stir in rhubarb sauce and mix well; add nuts and coconut. Spread on 8-inch square warm cake still in the pan, and broil until slightly browned. Leftover frosting may be spread on graham crackers and broiled for a children's treat.
Variation: Cream in 1 tablespoon of peanut butter with the margarine and sugar.

Chocafé Cake Filling

Chocolate chips   ¾ cup
Instant coffee powder   2 to 3 tablespoons
Sugar   ¼ cup
Rhubarb sauce (see Index)   ½ cup sweetened and drained
Egg yolks   3
Margarine   ⅓ cup, soft
Cream cheese   1 3-ounce package, beaten until fluffy

In the top of double boiler over boiling water, mix the first 4 ingredients, stirring until smooth; remove from heat. Beat in 1 egg yolk at a time. Return to double boiler and reheat over boiling water, stirring until thick. Beat in margarine. Remove from heat and continue beating until thick and smooth. Stir in cream cheese until well mixed. Spread between 2 layers of cake.

Fruity Fudge Frosting

Unsweetened baking chocolate 1 1-ounce square, grated
Semisweet chocolate chips 4 ounces
Sherry or rum 3 tablespoons
Salt pinch
Powdered sugar 3 cups
Rhubarb sauce (see Index) ¼ cup unsweetened and drained

In the top of double boiler over boiling water, melt the chocolate square and chips with sherry and salt. Remove from heat. Beat in about ¾ cup of powdered sugar, adding rhubarb sauce gradually as it stiffens. Beat for a minute to blend. Then gradually beat in the rest of the powdered sugar until it is stiff enough to spread. You may need less sugar, depending on the consistency of rhubarb sauce. Enough for top and sides of 8-inch layer cake.
Variation: You can make this frosting into fudge by adding ¼ cup raisins and ¼ cup chopped nuts. Spread on buttered plate and keep in refrigerator.

Pink Velvet Crème

Margarine 6 tablespoons
Powdered sugar 2 cups sifted
Salt ⅛ teaspoon
Cream of tartar ¼ teaspoon
Milk 2 tablespoons
Rhubarb sauce (see Index) ¼ cup sweetened and drained

Cream together margarine, sugar, salt, and cream of tartar. Add milk and beat at low speed of electric mixer. Add rhubarb sauce 1 tablespoon at a time, continuing beating until mixture is very light. Beat for 10 to 20 minutes. Spread between 2 layers of cake.

Honeyed Cream Sauce

Egg 1
Honey ¼ cup
Sherry 3 tablespoons
Rhubarb sauce (see Index) ⅓ cup moderately sweetened and
    drained
Margarine 1 tablespoon
Salt dash
Frozen orange juice concentrate 1 tablespoon
Orange peel ¼ teaspoon grated
Lemon juice 1 tablespoon
Nutmeg ¼ teaspoon
Evaporated milk 3 tablespoons

Break egg in top of double boiler. Beat with rotary beater until
foamy. Add honey, sherry, and rhubarb sauce, and beat well. Place
over boiling water, and add other ingredients 1 at a time, beating
with rotary beater after adding each one. Cook for about 10 minutes,
beating occasionally. Serve warm or cold over cakes, puddings,
fresh fruit. Store in refrigerator. Makes about 1 cup.

Strawberry Shortcake Sauce Supreme

Unflavored yogurt 1 cup
Whipping cream 2 cups, whipped
Rhubarb sauce (see Index) ⅓ cup sweetened and drained
Lemon juice ½ teaspoon

Fold the yogurt into the whipped cream. Mix in the rhubarb sauce
and lemon juice. Makes about 2½ cups.

Note: Combine this sauce with strawberries for an excellent accompaniment to
shortcake. The sauce also keeps well in the refrigerator.

Dessert Sauce au Vin

Sugar ¾ cup
Rhubarb 2 cups finely diced
Burgundy wine or dry red wine ½ cup
Ginger ¼ teaspoon
Orange peel 1 teaspoon grated
Cornstarch 1 teaspoon
Water

Sprinkle sugar over rhubarb and let stand for at least 1 hour, stirring occasionally. Add wine, ginger, and grated peel. Mix cornstarch with a little water until smooth, and add. Simmer until sauce is clear and rhubarb is tender; cover pan and let cool. Delicious over cakes, puddings, French toast, and pancakes. Or serve it as rhubarb sauce. Makes about 1½ cups.

Brown Sugar Sauce

Brown sugar 1 cup
Evaporated milk ¼ cup
Margarine 2 teaspoons
Salt ⅛ teaspoon
Rhubarb ⅓ cup finely diced
Raisins 2 tablespoons

Mix sugar and milk together well. Add other ingredients and simmer over low heat until rhubarb is barely tender. Serve over puddings and cakes. Makes about 1 cup.

Festive Fudge Sundae Sauce

Evaporated milk   ½ cup
Sugar   ¼ cup
Unsweetened baking chocolate   1 1-ounce square
Margarine   1 tablespoon
Rhubarb   ⅓ cup finely diced

Mix all ingredients together and cook in double boiler over boiling water, stirring occasionally, for about 25 minutes. Pour over cream puffs, ice cream, and puddings. Makes about 1 cup.

Mint Magic

Rhubarb   1 ½ cups finely diced
Sugar   1 cup
Fresh mint sprigs   8, very finely chopped
Tarragon vinegar   ½ cup

Let rhubarb stand in sugar for 1 hour or more. Mix in mint and vinegar; simmer for 20 minutes. Makes about 2 cups.

Note: A delicious sauce for lamb.

Always-on-Sundae Sauce

Rhubarb   2 cups finely diced
Sugar   1 cup
Large marshmallows   2, cut in thirds
Fresh strawberries   1 cup sliced*
Vanilla ice cream   1 quart
Slivered almonds   ⅓ cup toasted

Soak rhubarb in sugar for 1 hour or more. Add marshmallows and bring to a boil. Simmer only until marshmallows are melted. Chill well; then add berries. Serve ice cream in sherbet cups. Pour sauce over each serving and garnish with almonds. Serves 6.

*Crushed pineapple may be added in place of the berries.

Surprise Dessert Topping

Honey   ¼ cup
Mayonnaise   ¼ cup
Unflavored yogurt   ½ cup
Rhubarb sauce (see Index)   ¼ cup sweetened and drained
Shredded coconut   ¼ cup toasted lightly
Slivered almonds   ¼ cup blanched and toasted

Mix all ingredients together. Serve over strawberries, cake, or pudding. Makes about 1½ cups.

Candied Rhubarb Serendipity

Rhubarb   1½ cups finely diced
Sugar   1½ cups

Let rhubarb stand in sugar, stirring occasionally, for 6 to 8 hours or overnight. Simmer slowly, without stirring, until syrup has almost boiled away; let cool without stirring. Makes a chewy fruit that is delicious on ice cream or over cake, or added to other desserts. Makes 1 cup.

Pale Pink Syrup

Rhubarb purée (see Index)   ¾ cup sweetened
Light corn syrup   ½ cup
Honey   2 tablespoons
Margarine   1 tablespoon
Lemon juice   1 teaspoon
Lemon peel   1 teaspoon grated
Vanilla   ½ teaspoon
Cinnamon   ¼ teaspoon
Nutmeg   ⅛ teaspoon
Cornstarch   1 teaspoon
Cold water
Rum or sherry   1 to 2 tablespoons

Simmer together all ingredients but last 3 for 10 minutes. Dissolve cornstarch in a little cold water and stir into mixture. Then add rum. Good on hotcakes, puddings, or cakes. Makes 1½ cups.

Index

Appetizers
  Beanbarb Bash, 22
  Chafing Dish Mustard Dip, 23
  Egg Spread Exotique, 21
  Fresh Fruit Smorgasbord Dip, 20
  Ham and Celery Stuffer, 23
  Indonesian Vegetable Dip, 20
  Lemony Tuna-Barb Spread, 22
  Puget Sound Special, 21
Beverages
  California Waker-Upper, 25
  Eggstra Good Eggnog, 26
  In-the-Pink Health Drink, 26
  Mock Pink Champagne, 25
  Passionate Pink Punch, 24
  Pine-Barb Shake, 26
  Pink Pearl Froth, 25
  Rhubi Supercooler, 24
  Rosy Rhubarb Liqueur, 27
Breads
  Broiled Breakfast Buns, 35
  Brown Bread Bostonian, 28-29
  Busy Day Batter Buns, 34
  Cornbread à l'Orange, 28
  Deviled Quick Bread, 30
  Good Morning Coffee Cake, 32
  Ricky's Upside Downers, 33
  Spice-of-Life Muffins, 31
  Springtime Breakfast Bread, 27
  Tea 'n' Coffee Bread, 29
Breakfasts
  Golden Glow French Toast, 35
  Hallelujah Hot Cakes, 36
  Hearty Scotch Breakfast, 36
Cakes
  Cathy's Canadian Cupcakes, 141
  Chocolate Velvet, 142
  Deep South Yam Cake, 145
  Gingery Graham Cake, 146
  McIntire Oatmeal Cake, 143
  Never-Fail Spice Cake, 148

  Sour Cream Dream Cake, 144
  Spring Tonic Cake, 147
Candy
  Cocobarbary Bars, 121
  Fabulous Fridge Fudge, 120
  Fandango Nut Balls, 120
  Pieces of 'Ade, 121
Canning rhubarb, 17
Coconut milk, 101
Cookies
  Chewy Overnight Chocobarbs, 114
  Crunchy Drops, 119
  Del's Date Dainties, 118
  Drops Waikiki, 113
  Lemony Rhubarb Glories, 116
  Old-Fashioned Ginger Cookies, 117
  Rick's Rapid Rhubars, 116
  Rich Rhubarb Squares, 114
  Whole Wheat Chocolate Chippies, 112
  Zucchinied Sour Cream Squares, 115
Cooking rhubarb, 14-16
Desserts
  Banana Jubilee, 127
  Chocolate Rhubarb Imperiale, 127
  Danish Fluff, 124
  Rhubarb Delicioso, 125
  Rice Pudding Extraordinaire, 126
  Robbie's Rhubarb Refresher, 125
  Sauced Strawberry Amandine, 128
  Spring-in-a-Dish Compote, 122
  Winey Brown Barby, 123
  Yorkshireman's Delight, 122
  Frozen desserts
    Butter Pecan Sherried Ice Cream, 129
    Frosted Avocado Brasilia, 130
    Frosty Wine Sherbet, 131
    Regina's Doce Brasileiro, 128
    Rhubarb Crème, 132
    Rhubarb Ice Ana Maria, 131
    Sherried Rhuberry, 129
    Soft Frozen Velvet, 130

Ummmmmm Popsicles, 131
Dressing, salad
    Dieters' Salad Dressing, 54
Fillings. *See* Frostings
Freezing rhubarb, 17
Frostings
    Chocafé Cake Filling, 150
    Crunchy Fill-or-Frost, 149
    Fruity Fudge Frosting, 151
    Pink Velvet Crème, 151
    Quick Rhubarb Royale, 150
    Sweet-Sour Filling, 149
Growing rhubarb, 11-13
Jams
    Berry Good Jam, 75
    Burgundy-Barb, 75
    Glorified Rhubi Conserve, 76
    Jean's Jam Superbe, 76
    Marmalade Hawaiiana, 77
    Piquant Pepper Jam, 77
    Raspbarby Jam, 75
    Winey Rhubarb Jelly-Jam, 78
Juice, rhubarb, 16
Main dishes
    Meat
        Beef Broil Dijon, 80
        Bon Vivant Meatballs, 87
        Chilean Corn-Meat Pie, 83
        Curried Pork Supreme, 90
        Devilishly Delicious Lamb Steaks, 92
        Ginger Crumbled Ham, 89
        Lamb Piquant, 93
        Pork Chops Epicurean, 91
        Rhubarbeque Stew, 85
        Sauerbarb Patties, 81
        Sherried Ham 'n' Sweets, 89
        Sherried Onion Skillet Supper, 88
        Spiced Beef Special, 86
        Sweet-Sour Rhuburger Balls, 82
        Tart Layered Burgers, 84
    Meatless
        Bazaar Noodles, 107
        Brunch Eggs Guadalajara, 105
        Budget Garbanzo Cutlets, 109
        Fantastic Fromage, 106
        Fruited Lentil Beanpot, 107
        Louisiana Dinner Eggs, 104
        Pilaf Plus, 108

Red, White, and Green Rice, 110
Triple Bean Bake, 108-9
Whipped Cream-Cheese
    Omelet, 106
Poultry
    Burgundy-Barb Chicken, 98
    Deviled Chicken, 94
    Fred's Fruity Fowl, 96
    Ground Turkey Gustoso, 95
    Tart 'n' Spicy Turkey Legs, 97
    Wine-Curried Chicken Breasts, 99
Seafood
    Cantonese Cucumber Shrimp, 103
    Flavory Stuffed Fillets, 102
    Halibut Hullabaloo, 100
    Shrimp Baiana, 101
Pies
    Arabian Night Delight, 138
    Cloud Nine Raisin Chiffon, 138
    Marilyn's Mincemeat Deluxe, 133
    Piquant Citrus Pie, 140
    Pluperfect Berry Pie, 136
    Savannah Sweet Potato Pie, 139
    "See Red" Cream Pie, 137
    Sour Cream Cheese Pie, 134
    Spring Pie Supreme, 135
Purée, rhubarb, 16
Relishes
    Instant Meat Relish, 73
    Mustardy Meat Relish, 72
    New Zealand Rhubarb Chutney, 74
    Savory Catsup, 72
    Scandinavian Relish au Vin, 73
Salads
    Dilled Beet Salad, 51
    One-Dish Six-Boy Curry Salad, 50
    Pea Salad Confetti, 53
    Picnic Potato Salad, 47
    Raw Rhubarb Royale, 51
    Rhubarbarously Good Macaroni
    Salad, 52
    Springtime Salad, 48
    Sweetly Sour Cukes, 52
    Tangy Tuna Toss, 46
    Whipped Avocado Surprise, 53
    Wonderful Waldorf, 49
Sandwiches
    After School Special, 43

Cheesy Cucumber Open-Faces, 42
Glorified Gobbler, 46
Hearty Bacon 'n' Eggwich, 42
Layered Surprise, 44
Lo-Cal Cottage Sandwich, 44
Peanut Butter Broil, 45
Tangy Chickenwich, 45
Turkey Bombay, 43
Whipped Cream Cheese
  Sandwiches, 41
Sauce, rhubarb, 14-16
Sauces
  Dessert
    Always-on-Sundae Sauce, 154
    Brown Sugar Sauce, 153
    Candied Rhubarb Serendipity, 155
    Dessert Sauce au Vin, 153
    Festive Fudge Sundae Sauce, 154
    Honeyed Cream Sauce, 152
    Mint Magic, 154
    Pale Pink Syrup, 156
    Strawberry Shortcake Sauce
      Supreme, 152
    Surprise Dessert Topping, 155
  Meat and vegetable
    Avocado Nectar, 66
    Continental Caper, 67
    Sauced Onions Dijon, 66
    Savory Seafood or Salad Sauce, 65
    Three Savory Ham Sauces, 68
    Zesty Meat Sauce, 67
Soups
  Chilled Chicken Delight, 41
  Double Surprise Soup, 38
  Rhubarb Soup à la Zorba, 38
  Seafood Avocado Chiller, 39
  Viking Fruit Soup, 40
Stuffings
  Fruited Pilaf Stuffing, 70
  Toasty Cheese Stuffing, 69
Vegetables
  Be-Deviled Beets, 56
  Braised Onions Deluxe, 57
  Creamy Cooked Cukes, 60
  Double Red Beets, 56
  Fancy Smothered Carrots, 62
  Festive Corn Fritters, 59
  Gilded Broccoli Amandine, 63

Holiday Sweet Potato Nests, 62
Nutty Sweet Potato Puffs, 61
Party Rice, 63
Pea and Carrot Caper, 65
Rhubi-Red Sweet-Sour Cabbage, 57
Savory Pepper Fry, 58
Sherried Zucchini Gourmand, 61
Zesty Zucchini, 64

Other Books from Pacific Search Press

Asparagus: The Sparrowgrass Cookbook by Autumn Stanley
Bone Appétit! Natural Food for Pets by Frances Sheridan Goulart
Butterflies Afield in the Pacific Northwest by William Neill/
    Douglas Hepburn, photography
The Carrot Cookbook by Ann Saling
Cascade Companion by Susan Schwartz/Bob and Ira Spring,
    photography
Common Seaweeds of the Pacific Coast by J. Robert Waaland
The Crawfish Cookbook by Norma S. Upson
**Cross-Country Downhill and Other Nordic Mountain Skiing
    Techniques** by Steve Barnett
The Dogfish Cookbook by Russ Mohney
Fire and Ice: The Cascade Volcanoes by Stephen L. Harris
The Green Tomato Cookbook by Paula Simmons
Little Mammals of the Pacific Northwest by Ellen B. Kritzman
Living Shores of the Pacific Northwest by Lynwood Smith/Bernard
    Nist, photography
Make It and Take It: Homemade Gear for Camp and Trail
    by Russ Mohney
Messages from the Shore by Victor B. Scheffer
Minnie Rose Lovgreen's Recipe for Raising Chickens
    by Minnie Rose Lovgreen
The Salmon Cookbook by Jerry Dennon
Sleek & Savage: North America's Weasel Family
    by Delphine Haley
Spinning and Weaving with Wool by Paula Simmons
Why Wild Edibles? The Joys of Finding, Fixing, and Tasting
    by Russ Mohney
Wild Mushroom Recipes by Puget Sound Mycological Society
Wild Shrubs: Finding and Growing Your Own by Joy Spurr
The Zucchini Cookbook by Paula Simmons